To the beloved memory of my mother,
Gun Lundborg Cesarini, who translated this book.

Contents

Preface

Ever since I lived in Rome as a child, I have been interested in St Bridget of Sweden. It may have been taking part in the yearly celebrations on Boxing Day, organized by the Bridgettine Sisters for Scandinavians living in Rome, which first sparked my interest. When the Swedish Church in Rome was given its own place for worship in a chapel in the basement of the convent, the contact with the Sisters became even closer. Later, living in Sweden, I got in touch with some Bridgettine organizations, which led to an invitation to visit Rome for the celebration of the 600-year Jubilee of Bridget's Canonization.

My interest in this very special saint encouraged me to discover places in Rome which Bridget had visited or at least in some way had left her mark on. The result was a book on St Bridget's Rome. Once I had started researching, I kept finding more and more that was of interest.

During a scholarship year I spent at the Swedish Theological Institute in Jerusalem, I wrote a book entitled *The Return of St Bridget*. I read more books and articles, and attended conferences about her. My stay also gave me the opportunity to discover all the places that St Birgit visited during her stay in the Holy Land. My research resulted in the Swedish version of the book *With Birgit in the Holy Land*, followed by an Italian translation. Now it has finally been translated into English so that a larger public can be a part of St Bridget's exciting adventure. This book is the latest but hopefully not the last one, because Bridget is a woman who will never cease to interest and fascinate people.

I take this opportunity to thank my mother Gun Lundborg for the translation of this book, and it is my hope that *With Bridget in the Holy Land* will be used not only as a pilgrim guide but essentially as a means to see, understand and witness the life and writings of this extraordinary woman, and their ongoing significance for our own time. So, together with Bridget let us now approach the Holy Land!

Vadstena, 23 July 2023
650th anniversary of St Bridget's Celestial Birthday

1

The dream of the Holy Land

It was at the end of her life that Birgit Birgersdotter—Bridget in English—finally saw her dream come true: to journey to the Holy Land. It was from Rome, where Bridget had spent 22 years of her life, that she would begin, and her pilgrimage would become the great event of her life, resonating to our own day. On the way, she met many people, had revelations and visions, and confirmed her role as a prophet and spiritual guide. Her travels would also affect the way painters later represented Jesus' birth, crucifixion and descent from the cross. In spite of many misfortunes and dangers, the visit was a success, and almost everyone who had set out as part of Bridget's pilgrim party was later able to return to Rome.

The long-awaited message arrived on 25 May 1371. Some decades had elapsed since the first promise of a future journey to the Holy Land, and therefore the call to set out, pronounced as it were by Jesus himself, came quite unexpectedly: "You should now get ready to leave for a pilgrimage to Jerusalem to visit my tomb and other holy places. You have to leave Rome when I tell you."

All this may prompt several important questions. Why travel to the Holy Land? Why just Bridget? And why now and not earlier?

But let us start at the beginning.

In the course of her long life, Bridget would carry out many special tasks, which had been foretold by a priest in Rasbo at the time of her birth. One night in early summer 1303, he had a vision of the Blessed Virgin Mary who announced: "To Master Birger a daughter has been born, whose voice will be heard all over the world." Quite right. Not far from there, in Finsta House in Uppland, the same night, Birgit Birgersdotter was born. Her father, Birger Persson, was the region's administrator in Uppland. Her mother, Ingeborg Bengtsdotter, belonged to the wealthy royal Folkunga family. The priest's vision said that Bridget's revelations would be heard wherever she was and be spread abroad; her life and activities would be influenced by the revelations she received and the wide journeys she undertook.

As a small child after her mother's death, Bridget was taken to live with her Aunt Katarina in a place called Aspanäs at Lake Sommen in the region of Ostrogothia. At 13, she was married to Ulf Gudmarsson, who was a few years older and owner of the mansion Ulvåsa, south of Lake Boren. Bridget soon acquired a reputation as an enterprising housewife who put her gifts to good use. She built a hospital where poor people could receive treatment without charge and encouraged her husband to learn to read and write, so that they could pray the divine office together. Being able to read and write also meant that Ulf could continue his studies in canon and civil law, which for him opened the possibility to become a chief judge in the province of Närke.

Between the years 1319 and 1337, Bridget gave birth to eight children, five of whom would live to maturity. In the meantime, she had become a lady-in-waiting to the Flemish-born Queen Blanca, wife of the Swedish king Magnus Eriksson. Bridget was thus able to follow the court to different castles in Sweden and gain an insight into what was going on in the world.

Together Bridget and Ulf undertook two major pilgrimages. In 1339, they visited Nidaros Cathedral in Norway (now Trondheim), where King St Olof was buried, and the other one took them during the years 1341–3 to the tomb of the apostle James in Santiago de Compostela in north-west Spain. On their way back, they passed through northern France, which was badly damaged as a result of the Hundred Years' War. Reaching Arras, Ulf became ill.

Then, says Bridget, St Denise, the patron saint of France, revealed to her that Ulf would recover, which he did. In another revelation, Jesus revealed that God would speak through Bridget.

During their trip back to Sweden, shaken by the terrible experience of devastation and sickness, the couple decided to change their way of living. They moved to the monastery of Alvastra, where they lived in an annex and took part in the life of the convent. Ulf died some years later and was buried in the monastery church. Bridget decided to remain in Alvastra.

Now, during a period of five years called the "Time of Enlightenment", Bridget received numerous revelations and the prophecy that she should become God's spokesperson was also fulfilled. In one of them, she was told to start a new monastic rule called "The Holy Saviour's Order" to be located in Vadstena. But in order to establish it, she needed the pope's permission. Thus, Bridget decided to go to Rome and wait for the pope to return from his exile in Avignon. For Bridget, Rome was the only legal seat for the successors of St Peter.

Bridget arrived in Rome during the autumn of 1349. Her disappointment was great when she discovered the poor shape into which the Eternal City had fallen. Lawlessness, feuds and poverty prevailed in what once had been the most powerful city in the world. For this she blamed the pope's absence. Bridget sent him one written revelation after another, admonishing him to come back to Rome, with no immediate results.

During her first five years in Rome, she lived in a palace close to St Laurence in Damaso belonging to a cardinal, and later, for 19 years, she lived in a building nearby, called Palatium Magnum. Today it is called St Bridget's Home. While waiting for the pope to return, she visited places in and outside Rome, where she continued in her prophetic capacity to inform people of their false steps. Among them was the abbot in a Benedictine convent in the Sabine mountains, but also Queen Johanna in Naples was reproached for her way of life. Being an assiduous pilgrim, Bridget also visited the apostles' tombs in Ortona, Benevento, Amalfi and Salerno.

Finally in 1367, Pope Urban V (pope 1362–70) returned to Rome, and a year later the Roman Emperor Charles IV of Bohemia came to the city. Thus, the words sent her by Jesus just before her leaving Sweden came true: "Go to Rome, where you will see the pope and the emperor." After several meetings with the pope, which were not free from cultural clashes and linguistic confusions, Bridget's order was finally approved. However, in order to make her order legal, the pope had to bypass the Fourth Lateran Council of 1215, which did not allow new orders. Therefore he allowed Bridget to use the Augustine Rule, which with one addition became Bridgettine. Now she could consider her task accomplished and return to Vadstena. But what really kept her back in Rome was the disappointment of seeing the pope return to Avignon in September 1370, and that in spite of Bridget's premonitions. In any case, he died not long after. But when Bridget was still in Rome, trying to persuade the next pope, Gregorius XI (pope 1370–8) to move the court back to Rome, she came to know from a new revelation that the time was ready for her pilgrimage to the Holy Land.

2

Europe during Bridget's time

The fourteenth century was an extraordinary time, characterized by much unrest, plague, earthquakes and wars. The feudal system, which prevailed during great parts of the Middle Ages, had more or less collapsed, while numerous independent city states were formed. These small and newly formed states became new bases of power to be reckoned with, while the French and German-Roman era of greatness became a memory. The Church, in spite of its partly retained exclusive privileges, had lost its unique authority. The political map had now changed, causing constant conflicts between the pope and the emperor. Countries and even city states were divided between Ghibellines (who supported the Holy Roman Emperor) and Guelphs (who supported the pope). To make matters worse, the so-called Hundred Years' War between England and France began in 1337 and would last until 1453.

When we think of Europe during the fourteenth century, it is easy to give it a historic reality that is very different from ours. But is it really that way? Two world wars devastated the continent during the last century; smaller conflicts erupt in different places; catastrophes such as earthquakes and floods are regular phenomena, not to mention terrorism, climate change and huge economic crises. Among the similarities of our days, we can also include standardization. Europe during the fourteenth century had Latin as a lingua franca and most of the continent was held together under the leadership of the Church. As today, during the Middle Ages there was great co-operation between the countries in trade, culture and education.

Travel in the Middle Ages

It is difficult for us today to realize that people travelled a great deal during the Middle Ages, almost as much as we do today. Perhaps not everybody and not as often, but nonetheless similar distances were covered by many. Globalization and population surges during certain periods helps to explain why there could be an enormous stream of people travelling along the roads of Europe. Among them were soldiers, merchants and students, but there were also pilgrims, on journeys similar to those of tourists today. They travelled on foot, on horseback, in carriages and by sea.

For the Swedes, like Bridget, the main destinations were the sanctuaries built around the tombs of the saints both in and outside Sweden. This kind of travel was quite common, and the destinations were many. Bridget and her contemporaries visited places which are still popular today: Norway, Spain, Italy and the Holy Land.

Dreaming of the Holy Land

What was it that enticed pilgrims to travel such long distances? During the fourteenth century, many people felt a deep desire to do something concrete to show their faith or to make amends for their sins. Bad luck, such as a failed harvest, and epidemic diseases were considered a consequence of human disobedience and of failing truth. But asking for a saint's intercession or going on a pilgrimage to his or her tomb was generally believed to move God in order to find a cure for illnesses, misfortunes and famine. A pilgrimage could also be a way of thanking God for prayers that had been answered.

During the Holy Year of 1300, which was the year the first jubilee was celebrated, Rome was visited by half a million pilgrims from all over Europe. At the time, the population of Europe was about 15 million people. But why did so many people travel so far when there were many holy places closer to home?

For example, St Erik was buried in Uppsala, St Brynolf in Skara, St Botvid in Stockholm, St Eskil in Eskilstuna, St Sigfrid in Växjö, St Ingrid in Skeninge, just to name a few of the local Swedish saints. But it was not only the remoteness and holiness of places that mattered, but the status of the place was also important. Local saints were declared holy by the local bishops rather than by the pope, and all the Swedish saints belonged to this category. Next, there were saints declared holy by the pope. But of greater significance than these were the tombs of the fathers of the early church and the apostles. And most important of all were the places in the Holy Land connected with Jesus' birth, death and resurrection.

A lucrative business

A great deal of trade took place along the pilgrimage routes and the places they led to. There were also "travel agencies", which took care of all the practical things such as stops overnight, boat transports and armour-bearers. All along the routes there were hostels where pilgrims could stay overnight. At the pilgrimage sites themselves, there were often markets where the pilgrims could buy souvenirs and badges to put on their clothes. There were also of course those with less than honest motivations, such as traders offering fake relics.

In other words, pilgrimage offered a profitable business proposition for many. Banks were able to expand in new and different ways, especially issuing vouchers to pilgrims so that they did not need to carry much money with them during the trip. But the pilgrimage trade was also lucrative for the Church itself: there were those who could not or did not want to travel all the way to a holy place. False certificates could be issued for them, and they could remain at home.

During certain periods, the stream of pilgrims heading to Jerusalem could be huge, sometimes a little too huge. The main beneficiaries of the often extortionate entrance fees to holy sites were Muslims, and so pilgrimages to places were the Church could more directly benefit were encouraged, such as to Rome. But to visit Jesus' tomb and the cave where he was born was the dream of many, not the least Bridget. Her ancestors, including her grandfather and great-grandfather, all had once in their lifetime braved the distance and the dangers of a long pilgrim journey and had returned home as heroes. For them, the dream of the Holy Land had become a reality.

After the Crusaders' catastrophic defeat in 1187, Christians were no longer under the obligation to visit the holy places and during certain periods the situation could be chaotic. It was around 1330 that the Franciscan friars—after a long period of absence—were allowed to return in order to reorganize pilgrim visits. But the area was not really at peace; as late as 1368, the king of Cyprus with a few boats had directed an attack against Alexandria in Egypt, naming it a crusade! That incident, if we can call it so, was hitting back at the Christians in the Holy Land. Twelve Franciscan friars from Jerusalem and four from Bethlehem were deported to Damascus, where they were left to die of starvation in prison. This increased the tension between the different groups, leading eventually to a status quo between Christians and Muslims. But as everybody could take advantage of the frail peace, so everybody also had to follow the unwritten rules of the game. The Muslim tax-assessors and travel organizers, who took the tourists on their boats from Venice, Genoa and Amalfi to Jaffa, could do good business. But happiest of all were the pilgrims, as it gave them an enormous status and great satisfaction to have visited the famous holy places.

Why Bridget?

Now it was Bridget's turn to travel. There are many questions around this pilgrimage. Why Bridget? Firstly, it was a question of status. Belonging to the royal family and being a wife, daughter and mother of judges of the court, it was expected that she should follow in her ancestors' footsteps. In Europe, there were only a few sacred places she had not visited. Therefore, a trip to the Holy Land would be another feather in her cap. But her main reason for the trip was very different: she wanted an answer to certain theological questions and also to follow the direct summons from Jesus and Mary to visit the holy places where Jesus was born, crucified, resurrected and where he ascended to heaven.

The reasons were good, but why was she, at her age, ready to travel so far and take so many risks? She was already 68 years old, so why did she not stay in Rome and regain her strength, then return to Vadstena to become an abbess in the convent she had consecrated earlier? The pope had recently approved the rules of her new convent, which was what she had wanted. But everything changed when the pope went back to Avignon, and Bridget felt that she could not return to her convent until the Holy Father had taken his curia back to Rome. But Bridget was also eminently practical, and as the pope's return to Rome had been delayed, she had enough time to undertake the trip to the Holy Land. But all this was not anything she was planning herself. As on many other occasions, she was also guided by a voice from above.

3

The promise of the Holy Land

Before her departure for the Holy Land, Bridget received five revelations that confirmed that she should go. The promises contained in them were repeated in different places and over three decades. Sometimes there was a long period between them, but as time went on, Bridget came closer to their fulfilment.

In Arras, on the way back from Santiago

The first time Bridget received a revelation to go to the Holy Land was in 1342 in Arras in France on her way back from a pilgrimage to Santiago de Compostela, when her husband Ulf suddenly became ill. It happened during the Hundred Years' War, which became a traumatic experience for the Gudmarsson couple. It was the first time they experienced the horror of a war with its destroyed villages and people dying on the battleground. It was a consolation for Bridget that she received a revelation from St Denise, the patron saint of France, promising her that Ulf should recover. Another revelation came from Jesus who told her she should become God's spokesperson. The third revelation came from Mary, who introduced herself as the "Mother of Sinners", telling her that "you shall come to the places where I lived physically and there, with your spiritual eyes, you shall see my Son".[1] Perhaps all this was a way to comfort Bridget, who was then very distressed about her husband's illness. But at that moment Bridget had other issues to deal with instead of planning a pilgrimage, and some time would pass before it would be possible for her to travel abroad.

---

[1] *Extravagantes*, Chapter 66.

Between Alvastra and Vadstena

Once back from their pilgrimage to Santiago and as a result of Ulf's recovery in Arras, the couple decided to move to the monastery at Alvastra, where they could be part of life in the convent. But soon after, in 1344, Ulf died and was buried there. His tomb can be seen today, even though the convent itself is now a ruin. Ulf's death was a turning point in Bridget's life, but she decided to remain in the convent where she had lived with her husband.

Alvastra's history dates back to 1143, when Cistercian monks from the French town of Clairvaux, invited by the Swedish king Sverker, arrived and founded an abbey. Even though not much is left of it today, one can still sense the Gothic structure, where King Sverker was buried. In the fourteenth century, when Bridget lived there, it was a thriving monastic community.

One day in late 1340, on her way to Vadstena, Bridget, on horseback, received the next revelation. In a vision, she saw a monk telling her to go to Jesus and to Mary. As soon as she arrived in Vadstena, Bridget wrote down the vision, which became Number 5 in the *Book of Questions*. In Chapter 13, the last one, she wrote down how she heard God giving the following promise: "I know of five places. Whoever reaches these places, if he comes free from self-conceit and is burning with love, shall receive the goodness and sweetness of God."[2]

There are explanations as to which places in the Holy Land are considered holy, but there is also the condition that the visit will be good for whoever comes with a mind free from self-conceit and burning with love. There is no doubt that Bridget could be lacking these virtues, especially when she was Queen Blanca's court lady, faced with all the temptations of vanity and selfishness that such a position could encourage. A good way to exercise virtue was to be reminded constantly of what was right.

What are these "five places"? They are mentioned in the book of Revelation. The first was a vessel. The second one represented a lion. The third was a lamb. The fourth one is symbolized by a snake and the

---

[2]   Book 5, Chapter 13.

fifth by an eagle. These symbols are very clearly explained. Their aim was educational.

The first one, the vessel, symbolizes the Virgin Mary's birthplace in Jerusalem. As Jesus' mother, Mary was like a vessel carrying her son. She was the container to create Jesus as a man, a human being.

The second one, a lion, is the place where Jesus was born, the Church of the Nativity in Bethlehem. The prophet Isaiah describes the Messiah as "the lion of Judah's lineage".

The third, the lamb, is Golgotha, the place where Jesus was crucified in the Church of the Holy Sepulchre. It was there that Jesus died as a sacrificial lamb, an innocent victim, replacing the temple offerings with himself. John the Baptist describes Jesus as a lamb, God's Lamb, taking away the sins of this world.

The fourth one, the snake, represents Jesus' tomb, which is also to be found in the Church of the Holy Sepulchre. Snakes are visible in the holes and fissures of the rock. The symbol refers also to Jesus' expiatory death on the cross, where the snake from antiquity was defeated. The last symbol, the eagle, is the place of Jesus' ascension; the summit of the Mount of Olives, where Jesus was taken up to heaven like an eagle, when his mission on earth was accomplished.

Bridget heard God saying: "Therefore, whoever comes to these places clean and with complete good will shall see and taste how sweet and glorious I am." And for Bridget he added: "When you come to these places, I will show you more."[3] But at the time Bridget was busy with the establishing of her community in Vadstena, and for that reason, the dream of the Holy Land was still far away in her mind.

The Cardinal's palace in St Laurent in Damaso

In 1349, Bridget went to Rome to wait for the pope to return. In Milan, the pope had excommunicated the Archbishop Giovanni Visconti, and as Bridget had taken sides with the pope, she was asked to live in a palace belonging to the pope's brother, Cardinal Hugo de Beaufort. She stayed

---

[3]   Book 5, Chapter 13.

there for five years. At the end of the fifteenth century, the palace was rebuilt and connected with the Church of St Laurent in Damaso. Inside the church, you can still find a few interesting articles from Bridget's time. In the chapel named Cappella del Crocifisso, on the right side of the main entrance, there is a crucifix in front of which Bridget prayed in the old church. About this crucifix, as many others in Rome, it is said that divine secrets had been revealed to those who prayed in front of it. On a wall hanging made around 1880, Bridget is depicted in the dress of order of the Poor Clares, a grey dress with a girdle. The artist was presumably under the impression, as was common at the time, that Bridget belonged to the Third Order of St Francis, a view not held by more recent scholarship. She did, however, have a close relationship with members of the First Order of St Francis, the Friars, and this would be important during her trip to the Holy Land.

Her daughter, Katarina of Vadstena, is depicted in the same chapel. Here the painter is correct; she is wearing the dress of Bridget's order. It was Katarina who took care of her mother's plans. She also became the first abbess in the convent in Vadstena founded by Bridget.

At the beginning of 1350, when Bridget still lived in the cardinal's palace, she received another revelation that she should go to the Holy Land, and it was concerned with her speculations concerning the virgin birth. Although Bridget was sometimes without a certain logic in her acting and thinking, she was very down to earth. Since she had given birth to eight children during her time as a mother in Ulvåsa, she knew what childbirth was like. Therefore it was not strange that she thought deeply about how Mary could have given birth and yet remained a virgin. In the main points of Christian doctrine, Bridget was orthodox, and so she did not really doubt that Christ had been born of a virgin, but like most of her contemporaries her understanding of this doctrine was literal. Mary told Bridget in a revelation that "because you love me with a love so immense, I therefore announce to you that you will go on a pilgrimage to the holy city of Jerusalem at the time when it pleases my Son. From there you will go to Bethlehem; and there I shall show you, at the very spot, the whole manner in which I gave birth to that same Son of mine, Jesus Christ; for so it has pleased him."[4]

So, once Bridget had travelled to Bethlehem, Mary would show Bridget how the whole birth took place. It was really a mark of favour that Bridget should be able to go to Bethlehem and there witness Jesus' birth in real time! But when would it happen? Mary said, "when my Son finds it appropriate". Mary meets Bridget's down-to-earth question with a similar down-to-earth answer, which can be summarized as "Come and see!"

In St Lawrence Outside the Walls

Bridget received the fourth revelation about the Holy Land when she was in the basilica of St Lawrence Outside the Walls. The church is the fifth of the so-called Seven Pilgrim Churches in Rome. Its architecture is unique, and its history is both long and turbulent. In fact, there are two churches, one from the fourth century, and the other from the sixth. They were built in a straight line, with their apses touching each other. Both churches were restored in the thirteenth century and at that time made into one church by demolishing the apses. After the bombing of Rome in 1943, the church was rebuilt without losing its ancient and medieval style.

The fourth-century basilica was rebuilt in order to preserve the relics of St Lawrence, a deacon who was burnt to death in 258 during the persecution under Emperor Valerius. The relics of St Stephen, the first Christian martyr who was stoned to death (Acts 7:54–8:1), were also buried in the same tomb. His relics were found in 417 and taken to the newly built Church of St Stephen in Jerusalem. Later they were moved to Byzantium and finally in 560 to Rome to be placed in the same stone tomb as those of St Lawrence. Bridget often visited this church. One day, when Bridget was there, a young earl was about to kidnap her daughter Katarina, who had accompanied her mother. Just before the earl made his move he was struck by blindness. Only after he had confessed his bad

---

[4]   Book 7, Chapter 1.

intentions to Bridget and Katarina did his sight come back. From that moment, he became a faithful friend and protector of the two women.

At the beginning of the 1350s, on another occasion, Bridget was back in the same church and kneeling in front of the tomb of St Stephen and St Lawrence she prayed: "Blessed are you Saint Stephen. You have gained the same merit as Saint Lawrence. As he preached to the pagans, you preached to the Jews and as Saint Lawrence endured the fire, you happily endured the stoning. For that reason you are praised as the foremost of all martyrs."[5]

Then St Stephen answered by expressing in words his way of salvation. First of all, he said, he received education from his parents, then from Jesus. He became a disciple of Christ. After the ascension, he devoted himself to the task that he had been assigned, to such a degree that he was ready to die for his truth. He also mentioned the three things that had been instrumental to his glory: his goodwill, the apostles' prayers, and Jesus' suffering and love. And as Bridget is moved by his glory, his prayer will help her to learn more about God, and God's spirit will stay with her. The revelation ends with the martyr's prediction: "You will reach Jerusalem until the place where I suffered."[6]

In Palatium Magnum, now St Bridget's House

Criticism of the pope, who refused to return to Rome, became more pronounced in Bridget's mind. For that reason, she was evicted from the cardinal's palace in 1354. However, she found new accommodation not far away, which belonged to her noble friend Francesca Papazurri. It was a two-storey house, the front of which was decorated with a portico with five columns. The house had three smaller buildings attached to it and a garden protected by a wall. On top of the wall was a small tower, which provided a view and also protection. The name of the house was Palatium Magnum, and it would be Bridget's and Katarina's home for the

5   Book 6, Chapter 108.
6   Book 6, Chapter 108.

next 19 years. Today it is known as Casa di Santa Bridgeta—St Bridget's House, where the Bridgettine Sisters run a guesthouse.

Of the original house, there are only Bridget's and Katarina's rooms and the prayer room left, all restored during the nineteenth century. Through reconstructions and additions, it has now become a house with big windows and straight lines according to the architecture of the eighteenth century. After the Reformation in Sweden in 1527, the house was used for different purposes until 1930, when it was returned to the Bridgettine Sisters through Elisabeth Hesselblad's care.

In the prayer room, there are many souvenirs and relics left by Bridget, including a pelvic girdle, and a vertebra and a thighbone belonging to Bridget, together with the tabletop on which she died on 23 July 1373. In the glazed hallway leading to the apartment, Bridget's hair shirt and cloak are displayed.

The years went by. But then the promise was given that the date of departure was within reach. "Get ready for your pilgrimage to Jerusalem to visit my tomb and other holy places there. You can leave Rome when I tell you",[7] were Jesus' eagerly awaited words to Bridget on 25 May 1371. The time had come. The only thing to do now was to prepare the trip and wait for the announcement of the date of departure.

---

[7]   Book 7, Chapter 6.

4

Preparing to go

"Why do you blame your age?"

This gratifying news was followed by reflection and some apprehension. Bridget realized that such a long and adventurous trip could not be without risks. And what did Jesus say? Yes, he had given her a strong, clear but also right answer at the right time: "Why do you blame your age? I am the creator of nature. I can debilitate and strengthen nature according to my wish."[8] Well, it was quite simple. So why worry? If Jesus commands the pilgrimage, he must also be sure that the journey will be accomplished in a satisfactory way. Not only that, he promised to guide the party to and from Jerusalem. Everybody would be provided with what was needed.

Fellow travellers and the luggage

Fortified by the answer, it was time to prepare the travelling plan and the luggage. The departure, it was decided, was to be on 25 November.

The travelling group, apart from Bridget, was composed of the Spanish bishop Alphonse de Jaén with his two Spanish maids, Prassede and Elvira; Bridget's friend Francesca Papazurri; and Bridget's confessors, Prior Petrus Olausson from Alvastra and Master Petrus Olausson from Skänninge. Two Swedish family chaplains, Magnus Petri and Gudmar Fredriksson, also joined the group. They would later become prior and general confessor in the Convent of Vadstena. Three of Bridget's children

---

[8]   Book 7, Chapter 9.

were also to join the travelling party: Katarina, who had lived with her mother in Rome since 1350, and her two sons, lawyers and regional administrators, Birger and Charles, who had just arrived from Sweden to join them and who would be declared Knights of the Holy Sepulchre in Jerusalem. Bridget's maid Catherine of Flanders was also part of the group. In all there were 12 people.

In spite of everything, Bridget was still worried. Not so much for herself, as Jesus had promised her that all would be well, but what would happen to the others accompanying her? Well, in a revelation that was never written down, she learned that all her travelling companions, less one, should come back. That is what she told her confessors before leaving and what they confirmed during the canonization process. She was to be correct; it must have been hard for her to know that one person would not return home. It would not take long for her to learn who that would be.

Bridget had to tell everybody what they should bring with them and most of all what they had to leave behind in Rome. Bishop Alphonse wanted to take his whole library with him but was prevented by Bridget from doing so. She gave him permission to take only a few of the most necessary books. It was good that she did, for when the boat had almost reached its destination, it capsized just outside Jaffa and all their luggage was lost.

Mediation among the Franciscans

Some days before they left, a Franciscan friar, Pietro di Trastevere, came to Bridget to seek her help with some theological questions that were on his mind. A dispute was just then going on between the pope and different factions within the Franciscan order. The "Spiritualists" preached and put into practice total poverty and rejected the idea of owning any property at all. They therefore fell into conflict not only with the Church leaders but also with other Franciscan groups. They also asserted that the pope was not the rightful pope and that the Communion administered by fallen priests could therefore not be valid. The Church answered then by accusing the Spiritualists of heresy. All the time there was a fear that all the other Franciscan movements would be judged likewise.

Bridget joined in, not only in order to help a friend in spiritual distress but also to try and diminish the tension in the Franciscan order. Unity was important, especially now that the Franciscan friars, since 1342, had received the responsible and delicate assignment to manage the holiest places in the Holy Land. So why not ask the Virgin Mary for help as she had done so many times in the past? This was also part of the preparations for the trip. Bridget was given the answer in what once had been a Roman temple, the Pantheon, consecrated in honour of the Virgin Mary. Mary's answer to Bridget would be brought to light during the pilgrimage and later be used as a basis to mitigate the conflicts among the Franciscan friars.

The Pantheon

Pantheon, which in Greek means "Temple of All Gods", was completed around AD 130. It replaced another older temple from 27 BC with the same name. It is a unique building. The present structure is original, as are its heavy bronze doors. Today it is difficult to look at Pantheon as a church, in spite of the fact that it was consecrated as such in 609, in honour of the Virgin Mary. The changes made inside the temple strengthen the ancient and solemn feelings that this splendid Roman temple gives. The statues of the gods have been removed and replaced by statues of saints and tomb monuments representing well-known figures such as Raphael with his fiancée Margarita Luti and the first two kings of Italy: Victor Emanuel II and Umberto I with their respective queens.

Its unique and timeless atmosphere takes one back in time. For almost two thousand years people have passed through these bronze doors and walked inside the same room. Let us go back to 24 November 1371, the day before Bridget's departure. We can imagine the slender and elderly Bridget who approaches the bronze doors at a rapid pace—something she had done many times before—enters, kneels and in ecstasy receives the revelation from the Virgin Mary. Perhaps, while doing so, she may have looked up at the round hole in the roof, the only source of light in the church.

The answer to Bridget's questions

Her questions to the Virgin Mary were many. What is happening regarding the fallen popes' authority? And regarding the heretical priests' validity in administering the sacraments? And if Jesus was without property, is it right to criticize the vestments of the men of the Church? How poor was Jesus? Or, was he not at all poor?

As an answer to the first question, the Virgin Mary affirmed that the popes who, after their death, ended up in hell, in spite of everything, were real popes and that their decisions were quite valid. "It is in fact true and catholic faith, that if a pope who is without heresy but in other respects is stained by many sins, or other bad deeds, these do not make him so bad that he cannot keep his full authority and entire power to hold and set free the souls. This authority he owns through the holy Peter and has obtained it from God Himself."[9]

Mary's judgement is hard when it comes to those who question the validity of the office, both where popes or priests are concerned, and who have not lived according to the doctrine and rule. At the same time, she emphasized the importance of unconditional forgiveness.

When it came to Jesus' personal property, Mary confessed that he had owned a tunic that she had woven. It was certain that Jesus was poor, but not as poor as the Spiritualists would have us believe. They had denied Jesus having any property during his life on earth, but this statement had been condemned by Pope John XXII (pope 1316–34) and Bridget thought in the same way. A woven tunic had a certain value. But as much as Bridget criticized the Spiritualists, in her revelation 4:33, she complained at the same time that most Franciscans now have possessions, "something that their rules prohibit and they are happier about their reprehensible richness than their honourable poverty. And

---

[9]   Book 7, Chapter 7.

they are boasting about the fact that their robes are made of the same expensive cloth as those of the bishops."[10]

In that way, the bishops get their share of reproofs from Bridget. She tried to be impartial in her criticism, which could fall upon both poor and rich, without taking into consideration either person or station in life. In other words, she pleaded for moderation, not only in clothing but also in food, drink and sleep: not too much but enough not to be too tired and slack when serving God. Bridget's diplomatic answer to the Franciscan monks can also be summarized thus: there is virtue in moderation in every sense!

Fortified in her belief, Bridget was ready to start her trip.

---

[10] Book 7, Chapter 7.

5

On the way to the Holy Land

First destination Naples

The departure

On 25 November 1371, it was finally time to leave. On the Via Appia, paved in 312 BC under the direction of the censor Appius Claudius Caecus, the group travelled south. The road not only connected Rome with southern Italy and Sicily, but was also used by traffic to the harbours on the eastern coast, which guaranteed a connection with Greece, Asia Minor and North Africa. Our travellers' destination was the harbour of Naples, about 200 kilometres southwards, and from there they were going to continue by boat. Earl Latino Orsini, a close friend of Bridget's and Katarina's, accompanied them for part of the way.

To Sermoneta

Their first stop was 60 kilometres south of Rome in the small stronghold of Sermoneta, situated on a hill only a few kilometres from the main road. They were still within the borders of the Papal States. The castle was managed by the Caetani family who, together with the Colonna and Orsini families, were one of the most powerful families in Rome and with whom Bridget was on friendly terms.

Many witnesses during the canonization process mentioned an event which took place when the company was about to leave Sermoneta. Bridget's maid, Catherine from Flanders, became ill with a high fever. What could they do? It would have been expensive and difficult to leave

her in the lodging in Sermoneta. But as the maid was very much looking
forward to going to the Holy Land, Bridget's Master Petrus of Skänninge
decided to ask Bridget to pray for the maid's recovery. He said that as
Bridget had such a respect for God, he should certainly listen to her
appeal. Bridget listened to Master Petrus, got down on her knees and
prayed for a long time with her arms stretched out and her face against
the floor. When she had finished, she called her maid, who came out from
her room with a smile on her lips, completely recovered!

To Terracina

The travellers continued their trip south through the Roman harbour
town of Terracina, which during the fourteenth century was a free city.
It was situated on the border between the Papal States and the kingdom
of Naples. To avoid influence from Naples, it aligned itself with the Papal
States.

There are no written sources or revelations connected with Bridget's
visit to this town. But a fresco in the cathedral and remains from the Via
Appia are enough to confirm that Bridget passed through Terracina, and
not only once, but every time during each trip to and from Naples. It was
a town that was very close to her heart.

The cathedral of Terracina is a unique pearl dating from 1074, built
in the Romanesque style and decorated with Corinthian capitals. The
Cosmati floor was added during the thirteenth century. Inside the
cathedral there is a special commemoration of Bridget. In 1989, when a
wall was being removed, on the left side of the high altar, in the northern
part of the apse behind the ambo, a fresco appeared. Painted in bright
colours it represented a young and beautiful woman with soft features. In
Latin was written Beata Bridgeta—Blessed Bridget—, which means that
the fresco was made before the time of Bridget's canonization in 1391,
and must have been made between 1375 and 1390. Bridget is sitting at a
desk with an open book. An angel is hovering over her, and she is ready to
write down the divine revelation Sermo Angelicus. It means The Angel's
Dictation, something that Bridget received some time between 1349 and

1354, when she lived in the cardinal's palace in Rome. Later it became
the matutin (morning prayers) of the Bridget's Sisters.

Visiting Queen Johanna in Naples

Some days later, the pilgrims reached Naples. Since 1288 it had been the
capital of the powerful kingdom of Sicily, which extended over the whole
southern part of the Italian peninsula and the island of Sicily. It had been
governed by the French dynasty of Anjou since 1266. The kingdom was
practically part of the Papal States and from 1309 closely connected with
the pope in Avignon and France. On the throne was Queen Johanna I
(1327–82), who was also the titular queen of Jerusalem. A visit to her
was therefore very important, not least because Queen Johanna was also
connected with the Holy Land, the focus of their journey.

The queen's life had been quite tempestuous. Exploited in various
gambles for power, she had also been subject to rumours which, true
or not, damaged her reputation. Her first husband, Prince Andreas of
Calabria (1327–45) was murdered in 1345. As their married life had not
been happy, many accused the queen for having been behind it. Her
second marriage, to Louis of Taranto (1320–62), was happier than the
first but was overshadowed by the attempt of her first husband's brother
to get her to abdicate. In 1362, she was widowed again and in 1363, she
married Jacob IV (1336–75), titular king of Majorca. But in a hurry to
win back his kingdom, he left Naples in 1365. It seems that he turned up
for a short period, while Bridget was in Naples, only to disappear again
for good. He died in Spain in 1375.

This was the situation when Bridget visited the queen. She had already
been in Naples for a long period between 1365 and 1367, during which
time the two women developed a deep reciprocal friendship and respect
for each other, even though their relationship was sometimes stormy and
argumentative. This time there were several questions to deal with. Five
years had passed since Bridget's last visit and many things had happened
since then. Now Johanna was again in a difficult position. It was possible
that the queen had been accused wrongly, a result of plots and power
games, though she was not blameless. Both the queen and Archbishop

Bernhard of Naples were hoping that Bridget would give them her advice about some of the spiritual questions on their minds. She had therefore three revelations concerning the matter.

Revelations about Queen Johanna

Bridget's first revelation concerned Queen Johanna and started with a religious contemplation in which God the Father himself explains a series of problems. They are based in the free will of both angels and people: some angels chose evil and persuaded Adam to break God's commandments. After Jesus' expiatory death, the devil lost his total power and then those with free will could decide whether to follow God or the devil. God would decide which souls could be delivered from evil and redeemed. There is thus a battle between God, who wants the people to follow his will, and the devil, who wants them to follow their own desires. The revelation continues by unmasking the queen's deeds but suddenly stops. It may be that Bishop Alphonse tactfully censored the rest of it.[11]

Uncensored, the revelation describes the queen's decadence in graphic terms. It says that Bridget saw a woman dressed only in a shift, covered with semen and dirt. She also heard a voice saying: "This is a monkey sniffing her own posterior, with poison in her heart, who is causing herself damage and who is rushing into snares that cause her to fall!"[12]

The revelation gives a sombre picture of a powerful queen. Bridget this time did not speak for herself; she was acting as the intermediary of a revelation and she related what she saw and heard. This explains the raw choice of words, which were inappropriate for a noble woman like Bridget, who could be sharp and reprimanding without having to use this kind of language. The positive aspect of this horrible description is that when one has fallen to rock bottom, the only thing to do is to get up again. Therefore Christ is encouraging the queen, through Bridget, to confess. But that is not enough. The queen should also reign fairly,

---

[11]   Book 7, Chapter 11.
[12]   Book 7, Chapter 11.

pay her debts and not burden the people with newly invented additional taxes. The spiritual advice was given in 14 different points.

There are some direct exhortations about how the queen should deal with the people close to her; the revelation mentions the merchant Antonio di Carleto, later in the queen's service, advising her to promote him to a higher rank, even though that could be dangerous for himself and those around him. We do not know whether the queen followed this advice. In the same revelation, other people close to the queen also received good advice. One of them was Gomez Garcias de Albornoz, a diplomat and field marshal who died in 1380. He learned in part how to handle both his marriage and the finances of the country, and was told that he should become involved in military matters only if he was sure he was right.

Archbishop Bernard and the celibacy of priests

And now it was Archbishop of Naples Bernard III's turn. (He was archbishop from 1368 to 1378.) In two long and detailed revelations, the archbishop was advised to be moderate in everything; not to have more servants than necessary, to have not more than three changes of dress; to be frugal with food and not to own over-large horses; the horses were needed more for the defence of the country's borders rather than a display of one's vanity. The archbishop was to live in a more modest way, in line with the Franciscan belief about the poverty of the Church. It was something that Bridget followed in spite of her high social standing.[13]

Bridget disliked the archbishop's statement that "if he had been a pope, he would have allowed priests to marry". His argument was that marriage should be a way of avoiding the widespread loose way of living among the priests. But Bridget did not agree. It was true, she admitted, that priests could marry during the first centuries of the Church. It could therefore be justified in a theological way. But Bridget wanted to maintain the current

---

[13]   Book 7, Chapter 12.

rule of the Church, in spite of her constant criticism of the popes and others of high station within it.[14]

The son Charles

The visit to Naples was characterized by what happened to Bridget's son, Charles. It is said that during the trip, Bridget had told her children about manners and customs in southern countries. According to the rules of the court, a king or a queen should be kissed on their foot. In Naples—according to Margareta Klausdotter, a fifteenth-century abbess of Vadstena—Bridget's son Charles had caused a terrible scandal, by completing the kiss on the foot with another passionate kiss on the queen's mouth. It seems that the queen admired his courage and took a liking to him. According to the story, the queen wanted to prevent Charles from leaving against the promise that he could marry her. In any case, he was invited to her summer residence in Aversa at five kilometres north of Naples. The story told by Klausdotter is somewhat questionable and probably an invention of a later period; both Charles and the queen were already married, although not to each other, and if he really had been in love with the queen, he would certainly have behaved in a more discreet and diplomatic way.

The love affair—if there really was one—seems to have been very short-lived. On 24 February, Charles became ill. Already on his arrival in Rome he had suffered a violent haemoptysis, which people during the Middle Ages interpreted to mean that their hearts were soiled by sin. Bridget, upon his arrival, had met him, touched his heart and exclaimed with reproach: "Oh that heart!" At the same moment, Charles fell to the ground. Catherine explained to the people in the house that "my brother has arrived here in a miserable state. That is why God wanted to perform this miracle." Catherine's cryptic statement alluded certainly to Charles' many sins and for that reason God wanted, through the haemoptysis, to show where the problem was. Now he was on his way to the Holy Land,

---

[14] Book 7, Chapter 10.

which would be good for his soul. But sadly he never reached it. His
health deteriorated, and he died on 12 March 1372.

Charles' funeral

Charles had an elaborate funeral in the Church of the Holy Cross,
attended by many people. Even Queen Johanna's husband was present,
perhaps concerned about the rumours of his wife's alleged love affair.

During the funeral, Bridget approached her son's bier and said: "Go,
my son pilgrim, blessed by God and by me." Many of the guests at the
funeral were curious about Bridget's behaviour. She did not cry, and one
of the guests asked her if she did not grieve for the loss of her son. She
replied, "No, even if I knew that he should be the ruler of the whole earth,
I would not want him back to the misery of this life."

The reason why Bridget reacted in this way arose from the fact that
her heart was at peace. Death had put a stop to Charles' illicit relationship
with the queen; something had certainly happened between them.
And this was how Charles' time of grace had ended. Nobody could do
anything about it. That Charles was later promoted to the glory of heaven
was something that Bridget later got to know about in Jerusalem.

After the sad events of Charles' death and burial, there was nothing
to hold the company back in Naples.

6

On the stormy sea

Messina

On 14 March, the last Sunday in Lent, the boat left harbour going south along the west coast of Italy, passing by the towns of Amalfi and Salerno. Seeing these vibrant towns with their splendid domes, Bridget probably remembered her pilgrimage to the tombs of the apostles Andrew and Matthew in 1366. Now she was going to the land from where they had been sent in order to "go and make disciples of all nations", to quote Jesus' words in Matthew's Gospel. The boat continued to the Sicilian harbour of Messina. It is situated on the other side of the Sound of Messina, connecting Sicily with the mainland. They arrived there on 19 March, but there they had to wait a whole week for a more favourable wind in order to continue. On 21 March, they celebrated Palm Sunday in the Cathedral of Messina. Built in 1160, the cathedral miraculously escaped damage many years later from the devastating earthquake that destroyed the town in 1908.

On Good Friday, 26 March, the weather improved so that the company could set sail in the direction of Cyprus.

Storm-tossed through the Ionic and Aegean Seas

The trip to Cyprus continued in stormy weather and the group had to stop at several harbours to seek refuge before they reached their next destination. They visited places which today are well-known and popular tourist resorts, associated with Greek mythology and connected with the early years of the Church. Unfortunately sailing through the

Mediterranean Sea was dramatic and far from glamorous and relaxing. However, in spite of this, they never heard Bridget complain, according to the testimonies during her canonization process. On the contrary, she praised and thanked God that she was worthy to endure such afflictions!

On 30 March, the boat reached the island of Kefalonia in the Ionic Sea, a place characterized by Greek mythology. The island is situated across the Gulf of Patras and separated from Ithaka by the seven-kilometre-long Strait of Viskardo. Since AD 395, it had belonged to the Eastern Roman Empire, and when the Latin Empire was established in 1204, it came under the protective wing of the Venetian Republic.

On 1 April, late at night after having said their evening prayers, it was time for the pilgrims to sail again.

All these indications of places and dates come from one of the travellers, Bishop Alphonse, who kept very detailed daily notes. He also wrote that on Sunday 4 April, the boat went off course. They did not know where they were, until one day later when it was possible to land at the island of Kos, north-east of Rhodes.

The island of Rhodes had been governed since 1315 by the Johannite Order (also called the Order of Malta), founded in 1099, whose original aim was to protect pilgrims. When the last Christian town in the Holy Land was lost, the Order moved its headquarters to Cyprus. But as the Order needed its own territory, after some negotiations with the Byzantine Emperor, it was given permission to govern the island of Rhodes.

The apostle Paul visited Kos during one of his trips, and some of the first Greek churches were built there. In Acts 21:1, Luke describes Paul's visit to the island: "When we had parted from them and set sail, we came by a straight course to Cos, and the next day to Rhodes, and from there to Patara."

The revelations about the ship and the sea

To travel by boat on a stormy sea has always been an unnerving experience. But Bridget was not afraid; as usual she was reassured by what she saw and heard. It was Jesus who, in the middle of the turbulent sea, said to her: "Listen to me, you who are longing for a harbour after the tempests of the world! Nobody at sea has to be worried if I am with them."[15] He compared the ship to a person who is pushing through the stormy sea of life, propelled by free will. But he or she who is longing for God's words can also count upon God's presence in the boat, so that the dangerous rocks, which put obstacles in the way, will be harmless.

In another revelation, the ship is compared to the world, "full of concerns and hurling by the stormy waves, without leaving humans any safety and peace before arriving at the harbour of rest".[16] The three parts of the ship are compared with the three epochs of the world: the bow is high and wonderful and represents the time before Jesus' birth, characterized by the patriarchs' piety, the prophets' wisdom and the following of the law. The middle part of the ship, being lower and more submissive than the other parts, represents the time after Jesus' birth. But as ungodliness took over and Jesus' suffering was almost forgotten, the third part is coming up. It represents Bridget's time until the end of the world. Through Bridget, God's word was sent to the world. Whoever follows it will be blessed.

In a third revelation, different attitudes are compared with three ships. In the first one, there are all those who give up their hope and live an undisciplined life. They have lost their rudder and are thrown towards the island of death.

On the second ship, which has a mast, a helm and an anchor, the main anchor is broken and the helm can easily come loose if the waves hurl themselves between the ship and the helm. And as in all parables, the main anchor is a life of purity and godliness. This anchor has become loose as the Father's instruction is no longer of any importance, and everybody is following their own rules. The second anchor is a willingness to follow God and is tied to two ropes: hope and faith. But if you love something more than God, the waves will come in, detaching the ropes. The boat will then begin to drift.

The third ship has all its equipment and is ready to leave when the time comes. That is where God's friends are present. So ends the revelation.[17]

---

[15]   Book 4, Chapter 44.

[16]   Book 6, Chapter 67.

[17]   Book 4, Chapter 88.

7

In Cyprus

In the harbour of Paphos

On 8 April, after three days on Kos, it was time to leave and continue the trip. This time the boat was able to reach Cyprus without any interruption. It arrived at the harbour of Paphos on 13 April. During the Greek-Roman days, Paphos was Cyprus' capital, famous for the ruins of the old Governor's Palace, where even today the elaborate and well-preserved mosaics are a great tourist attraction. There are also the Royal Tombs, so called not because of who is buried in them but because of their size and magnificence. Some of the tombs probably belonged to the aristocrats of Paphos. They were carved into the rock and dated back to Hellenistic and early Roman times. According to mythology, Paphos is the birthplace of the Greek goddess of love, Aphrodite. But for our travellers it was visited by the apostle Paul (then Saul) during one of his mission trips (Acts 13:6–7): "When they had gone through the whole island as far as Paphos, they met a certain magician, a Jewish false prophet, named Bar-Jesus. He was with the proconsul, Sergius Paulus, an intelligent man, who summoned Barnabas and Saul and wanted to hear the word of God."

In the capital Famagusta

Their next destination was the capital, Famagusta, on the eastern side of the island, where they arrived a day later, on 15 April, a Tuesday.

Cyprus has a surface of 9,250 square kilometres and is the third biggest island in the Mediterranean after Sicily and Sardinia. It is situated around

75 kilometres south of the southern coast of Turkey. Due to its strategic position, the history of Cyprus has during certain periods been stormy. The island had belonged to Rome during the years 58 BC–AD 1191 until King Richard the Lionheart conquered it on his way to the Holy Land during the Third Crusade. He sold the island one year later to the former king of Jerusalem, Guido de Lusignan, who established the kingdom of Cyprus. In 1489, it was the turn of the Republic of Venice to conquer the island. The Christian dominance ended abruptly in 1570, when the island was conquered by the Ottoman Empire.

At Queen Eleanor's Palace

When they arrived in the harbour at Famagusta, Bridget was received by Eleanor of Aragon (1333–1417), the queen regent of Cyprus and widow of King Peter I of the house of Lusignan (1328–69). The marriage between Eleanor and Peter had been arranged in 1353 in order to reinforce the power ambitions in the Mediterranean Sea. Eleanor's life had not been a happy one. In 1366, King Peter took part in a raid against Alexandria, which had bad consequences for the Franciscans in the Holy Land. Eleanor was appointed to govern Cyprus during her husband's absence, and she remained in this position for three years, as Peter after the crusade undertook a long trip to Europe. On his return to Cyprus in 1369, Eleanor was accused of having committed adultery with John of Morf, the titular prince of Edessa, though she was later acquitted.

Peter was not a popular king because of his despotic behaviour. Some plotted against him, probably his brothers John and James. On 17 October 1369, Peter was killed by three knights in his palace of La Cava in Nicosia. The queen's 12-year-old son Peter was then crowned King Peter II (1357–82), while Eleanor became a regent of Cyprus together with her brothers-in-law John and James, who had probably been involved in her husband's death! While Eleanor was struggling to save the throne for her son against his uncles, Bridget arrived in Cyprus.

The revelation for the people of Cyprus

It was a turbulent time when Bridget arrived, and therefore it was understandable why Eleanor, like Queen Johanna in Naples, wanted to hear Bridget's advice regarding the governing of the country as well as the problems of her family. The queen and Bridget withdrew to the queen's summer residence in Nicosia, and the queen unburdened herself by confiding in Bridget. As ever, we do not know exactly what was said, but reading between the lines of Bridget's answer, which came just before her departure, we can imagine the kind of conversation that took place. Once back in Famagusta, Bridget summoned the court and other people of standing and influence. In a long and exhorting speech, she told them what could happen if the people in Cyprus did not discipline themselves. Famagusta could be laid waste and its inhabitants taken away to die in a foreign country. The revelation was also directed towards the female aristocracy who, according to the fourteenth-century fashion, dressed in tight-fitting dresses with low necklines.

The revelation was also directed at Duke John, accused of murdering the king, who "aware of his brother's death, is bragging of his looseness and not about what he had done to his next of kin". Bridget predicts a worse death for him if he does not repent. Later the prophecy came true. The duke's confessor also came in for criticism: he was too complacent and relaxed towards the duke. "Such a confessor is a traitor," said Christ through Bridget. There was also admonitory advice to the queen and her son to forgive what had happened, to govern in all fairness, to have good advisors and not to impose useless taxes. The new king, she said, should not be blamed for his father's mistakes. "But now the governments are not governments but a child's play, foolishness and robbery. It is therefore important to have a king who is mature for his task, experienced, wise, just and hard-working and who loves his fellow-beings' use more than his own will." During this admonitory address she also promised to pray for them and to do penance as soon as she reached the Holy Land.[18]

---

[18]   Book 7, Chapter 16.

The response to the revelation

The responses to Bridget's words were of both praise and blame. Some people, like Simon, a Dominican friar, made fun of Bridget, saying that the old woman had gone mad. But others took her message seriously; some even wanted to join the pilgrimage. One of them was the queen's confessor, Martin of Aragon, a Franciscan friar. As a member of the Franciscan order, he had to follow the Franciscan rules, and this could be possible if he followed Bridget to the Holy Land. Once there she had a revelation reminding him, as he was a Franciscan, to follow the rule of St Francis. We also know that Martin returned some months later to Cyprus with some of Bridget's revelations addressed to the king of Cyprus and his people, to which we will return later. On his return to Cyprus, Martin gave away all his possessions of silver, jewels and money to the poor.[19]

Another person whose life was changed after having met Bridget was the English knight, William Williamson. In 1375, he left his place at the queen's court in order to end his days as a Franciscan friar in Bethlehem. There, his task was to guard the Church of the Nativity.

Leaving Cyprus

Bridget and her fellow pilgrims departed from Famagusta somewhat concerned after they had heard how dangerous it was for pilgrims to stay in the Holy Land. Bridget was even advised to blacken her face and dress as a Muslim woman. But in a revelation Jesus told her: "Don't let your clothing and face be changed and entrust your will to Me. As I saved Sara from the people who imprisoned her, I shall also take care of you in the best of ways both on the sea and on the land."[20]

At the beginning of May, the anchors were weighed and the company, now with one more passenger, finally sailed for the Holy Land.

---

[19]   Book 7, Chapter 20.
[20]   Book 7, Chapter 16.

8

In the Holy Land

The way to Jaffa

The distance from Cyprus to the mainland was about 200 nautical miles, and the voyage took several days. At the beginning, the weather was fine, but when the boat was within reach of the harbour of Jaffa, a storm began to blow up.

Did Bridget have huge expectations of the Holy Land, which she could now see from the boat? No, this time she had kept her expectations very low: she was well aware of how things stood at the moment. She knew that the situation was unstable and that the Muslim rulers were afraid that the Christians would try again to take control of the Holy Land. However, the situation had become better and thanks to some negotiations, the Christian pilgrims had permission to visit the holy places.

The Mamluk Sultanate

The Holy Land had been governed by many different people and countries. The Mamluks were originally slaves from the land around Caucasia east of the Black Sea. In 1240, in order to form the guard of the sultan of Egypt, thousands of them were bought and trained to use weapons. But only ten years later, through a state coup, they became the lords of Egypt. Their empire reached, among other countries, Palestine and Syria. In 1291, by conquering Acre, they destroyed the last remaining wreckage of the Western Christian domains. Their power was tested when they managed to defeat the Mongolian forces, which in 1300 had threatened Jerusalem. The Mamluk State remained until 1517, when the Ottomans took over and dominated the Middle East for several centuries.

The shipwreck

The Mamluks were not a problem for our pilgrims when they arrived in Jaffa, as many had feared; in fact, during their whole stay in the Holy Land, there is no mention of a confrontation with them. The biggest danger came instead from the forces of nature. Once close to the harbour of Jaffa, the weather became very bad and the boat foundered on the rocks at the entrance of the harbour.

The passengers were seized with panic and the Spanish maids wept in fear, but Bridget, with her usual calmness and practicality, assured the passengers that nobody would lose their life. She trusted the promise she had received in Rome that "all but one should come back". And the one was her son Charles, who had died in Naples.

Her prediction was correct. In spite of the fact that all their luggage was lost, all the passengers were able to go aboard a lifeboat, which took them the last 100 metres to safety. Bishop Alphonse must have felt grateful to Bridget, who had dissuaded him from taking his whole library with him! Now he knew that his books were safe back in Rome.

Jaffa

Jaffa is one of the oldest towns in the world. Today it is enclosed by the modern Tel Aviv, which was founded by Jewish settlers in 1909. It had then, as today, a very important harbour. The name of the town comes from Japheth, one of Noah's three sons. Another tradition, perhaps not so certain, is that the name derives from the Hebrew word for "beautiful", *yaffa*. Today, some of the reefs just beyond the harbour are no longer visible, since the British built over them in the 1930s. Only a few of them can be seen, but there are enough to get an idea of the dramatic shipwreck. One of the reefs left behind is, according to mythology, the so-called "Andromeda's reef", on which Andromeda, the daughter of

Jaffa's King Kepheus, was tied to be offered to a sea-monster to appease his wrath. But, says the legend, the hero Perseus, who was in love with the princess, happened to come by and killed the sea-monster. In that way, he saved Andromeda, who later became his wife, with the consequence that the inhabitants in Jaffa could breathe safely. Another story connected with Jaffa is the biblical narrative about Jonah, who for three days and nights was swallowed by a whale. As a memory of this event, there is a big sculpture of a whale in the centre of town. The story about Jonah will return in a revelation that Bridget had in Naples on her return, which was intended for Pope Gregory XI.[21]

Once landed, the pilgrims had no problems going ashore. The first thing they had to do was to pay the entrance ticket of five dirham to the harbour authorities and two dirham to the interpreter. Then everybody had to be registered. The authorities made a note of their bodily structure, height, colour of their skin and other distinguishing features. A Franciscan friar from Rama, then the capital of Palestine, was also present, to teach the pilgrims the written and unwritten rules of how to live in a Muslim country. Later he took them to a hostel, which was more of a campsite, as Jaffa and its harbour had been completely demolished in 1267, when conquered by the Egyptian sultan Baibars al Bunduqdari (1223–77). It was left in ruins until the seventeenth century in order to discourage prospective Crusaders from using the harbour as a base for a further conquest of Palestine.

The home of Simon the Tanner
and the Church of St Peter

The company remained a couple of days in Jaffa in order to recover from the long trip and the shock of the shipwreck. In the meantime, they were able to visit the house that tradition said was the home of Simon the Tanner, where the apostle Peter was a guest for a long time, after raising from death a woman named Tabitha (Acts 9:36 ff.). When staying there, Peter, in a revelation, saw a sheet with pictures of different animals

---

21   Book 4, Chapter 143.

and heard a voice confirming that it was permitted to slaughter and eat these animals (Acts 10:10 ff.). This was interpreted that no food should any more be considered impure. It also meant that non-Jews could be accepted by the Christian community. The house, though rebuilt, is still there. A family by the name of Zakarin lives there, so the closest you can come to the house today is the closed doors. On the arch on the entrance it is written in English in large letters: "House of Simon the Tanner".

Not far from there, in memory of the apostle Peter and his visit, the Church of St Peter was built in 1654 on the ruins of an old stronghold. It was destroyed twice and finally rebuilt in 1894.

From Jaffa to Jerusalem

The journey to Jerusalem took our pilgrims along the Old Jaffa Road. Through a deep valley the company reached Rama, some 20 kilometres to the east. Rama was a junction for caravans and a prosperous commercial town. It also had accommodation for pilgrims, managed by the Franciscans.

After one night of rest, they were able to continue through Lydda (today Lod) and Emmaus, the village where Jesus revealed himself after the resurrection to the travellers on the Emmaus road. In memory of this event, around the year 1100 the Crusaders built a Gothic church in the Burgundian style.

The closer our pilgrims came to Jerusalem, the more they had to climb, as the landscape becomes more mountainous. Jerusalem is situated high up, at 750 metres above sea level.

The all-inclusive Jerusalem pass

On 12 May, our pilgrims were finally able to enter the holy city of Jerusalem through the Jaffa Gate, but only after paying a tribute to the sultan of 72 dirham each or 4½ golden florins. It was quite a large amount, equal to 72 days' wages for a worker. However, the pilgrims now had an all-inclusive Jerusalem pass which allowed free entry to the shrines in the city.

Checking in

There is no doubt that Bridget's group was met by the custodian of Sion, who was then the Franciscan friar, Antonius di Giacomo, who was to help the pilgrims with their accommodation.

Once there they had to check in. There were three alternatives, which at the end proved to be two. One was a luxurious lodging in the Franciscan monastery on Sion, intended for people of a high status. In other words, appropriate for Bridget and the people she brought with her.

The other one was built as late as 1353 and situated close to the monastery, where, according to tradition, Jesus instituted the Eucharist. It was aimed to be used only by female pilgrims. This would also be a proper accommodation for Bridget and the women in her group. The only problem was that it had been confiscated six years earlier by the Egyptian authorities after the raid on Alexandria by the king of Cyprus, Peter I. In any case, a treaty had been signed on 29 September 1370. It was also known that Queen Johanna of Naples was going to pay a ransom in November 1372, equal to the value of the whole building. But as the restoration was not yet finished, this lodging was not so far an alternative for the pilgrims.

The third alternative was the Hospice of St John. It had been built by the merchants from Amalfi in 1060 and was situated just opposite the Church of the Holy Sepulchre. Being a very simple building, it had fallen into disrepair and was demolished during the sixteenth century to make room for the four-sided business-area known as Muristan.

The choice was therefore between the first and the third alternative. Bridget wondered: shall we live luxuriously or simply? As it had happened in the past, she asked Virgin Mary for advice and the answer came immediately. In a revelation, Virgin Mary pointed to the simpler place, saying that Bridget should stay there as a good example for other people. And who were the other people? It is possible that the revelation was aimed at the Franciscans who had failed to follow St Francis' effort to live a simple life, to live in comfort and luxury. But Mary promised that in the simple Hospice of St John, in spite of its standard, Jesus would take care of the pilgrims, so that they would not be in need of anything.[22]

---

22   Book 7, Chapter 70

9

The Church of the Holy Sepulchre

The first and most important destination for our pilgrims was just across the street: the church that had been built on the place associated with the core of Christian faith. Here you will find what has been described in the Book of Questions as the Lamb and the Snake. The church, with its irregular size, contains both Mount Calvary and Jesus' tomb. In the West, it is called the Church of the Holy Sepulchre, in the East the Church of Resurrection. The last is certainly a more correct name, as the Christian faith is based on Jesus' physical resurrection.

The original church was built by Emperor Constantine and dedicated in 335. His idea was to build a basilica according to a Roman design with five aisles. The only exception was that the choir was turned to the west and not to the east. As a rule, basilicas are built with the choir towards the east, towards Jerusalem, the place of Jesus' tomb. But this church was built in Jerusalem, and the choir was in fact turned towards Jesus' tomb situated just a few metres outside the apse in the west. A large area of the hill, where the tomb had been excavated, had been removed to leave only the tomb, covered by walls and a roof. Over the tomb, a round church had been built and named Anastasia Rotunda. Both Anastasia's and Constantine's basilicas were connected by a rectangular yard, fenced by a wall with an interior colonnade. On the inside, the Golgotha rock rose in the open air on the south-east corner.

Both the basilica and the rotunda were burnt down by the Persians in 614. They were restored but destroyed again in 1009 during the reign of the Muslim caliph al-Hakim bi-Amr Allahs (985–1021). Between 1099 and 1149, the Crusaders rebuilt the earlier churches from Constantine's time, enclosing them into one large and irregular church, including the yard of Mount Calvary. The entrance was moved from the eastern to the southern side, where once the yard had been. Since then, the church has maintained this structure, in spite of the fact that it was devastated by a fire in 1808 and by an earthquake in 1927 which caused great damage. The upper part of the bell tower had already been lost in 1545 in another earthquake and was never rebuilt. A mosaic over the entrance, depicting the Virgin Mary, and some columns in red, white and green porphyry around the porches have also disappeared, as well as reliefs from the white marble friezes over the doors. They depicted Lazarus' resurrection, Jesus' entry in Jerusalem, the institution of the Eucharist and Judas' kiss in the Garden of Gethsemane. In spite of the peeled front, the original structure from around 1100 has remained. The three cupolas have also survived: the largest is over Constantine's rotunda, the second over what once was Constantine's basilica, and the smallest one over Golgotha.

In spite of several reconstructions and extensions, the church is steeped in history and holiness. An unbroken tradition of faith demonstrates that it was here that the most holy of events took place. And it was with this feeling that our pilgrims from Rome came to the most holy of all holy places. They visited the church the day after their arrival in Jerusalem, very appropriately on a Friday, the day when Jesus was crucified and laid in the grave.

Opening hours

When Bridget visited the church, the keys were kept by eight Muslim civil servants. As there were three different locks with the keys distributed among three of them, preferably among all the eight, these three or eight had to be on the spot to open and close the church. And at every closure to put the seals in their right place and to check these every time that the church had to be opened. These instructions had been given by the Egyptian sultan As-Sálih Ayyúb (1205–49), when Jerusalem was taken back from the Crusaders.

Today there are two Muslim families, Joudeh and Nuseibeh, who have inherited the honour of keeping the keys to the church. It is a very practical solution, as the church, as at the time of St Bridget, is shared by several different church denominations, which do not always get on well together. Here you find the headquarters of the Greek-Orthodox Church and of the Armenian Apostolic Church. The Coptic-Orthodox Church, the Ethiopian-Orthodox and the Syrian-Orthodox Church also each take up one part of the building. This is regulated by the Status Quo, a decree from 1852, established by the Ottoman sultan. Yet the church has a common festival day for all these denominations. It is held to celebrate the Elevation of the Holy Cross on 14 September, the day when Constantine's mother Helena found the cross of Jesus.

When Bridget visited the church there were people outside selling the entrance tickets. They were sitting at small tables with small scales in front of them to control the weight of the gold and silver coins they were given. Bridget had already taken care of this at the Jaffa Gate. The church was open twice a day, in the morning between 6 and 9 am and later in the afternoon between 3 and 6 pm. After that, the door was closed and affixed with a seal.

If the church was closed or if the visitors did not have enough money to pay the entrance fee, it was possible for them to see it from the chapel on top of the staircase on the right side of the entrance, which was situated on the Golgotha hill. The chapel is identical with Station X of the cross, where Jesus was stripped of his garments.

Inside the church

The inside of the Church of the Holy Sepulchre today is very much the same as the one that existed during the Crusaders' time. It is a large irregular structure on different levels, and it covers several holy places connected with Jesus' suffering, death and resurrection.

The first thing you see when entering the church is the stone of the unction. The first known stone is from the twelfth century and the present one is dated 1810. It is at the place where, according to tradition, Jesus' body was anointed with oils and spices after being taken down from the cross. It is identical with Station XIII.

Once inside the church, our pilgrims were taken by the Franciscans to different holy places, where they were told the biblical texts associated with them. Then each person was left to choose a place where they could pray and contemplate. The low illumination and the peace inside the big basilica created a natural, devout atmosphere. It was common to allow the pilgrims to stay in the closed church overnight to enable them peacefully to say their prayers and meditate. Usually they brought food with them, bought from one of the many street-vendors. At night, they could also lie down and sleep on a pallet wherever they found a place.

The revelations about Charles' judgement

At the doorstep of the entrance to the church, Bridget received two very short revelations. They had both the same reassuring message, allowing a heavy weight to fall from Bridget's heart. Her son Charles, who had died in Naples in inauspicious circumstances, had been saved! The reason was in part thanks to Bridget's intercession connected with the pilgrimage, but also thanks to Charles' longing to undertake a pilgrimage to Jerusalem with the intention of being released from his sins.[23]

In the second revelation Mary tells Bridget that she was very close to Charles when he was about to die. For this reason, no bad thoughts could therefore defile him, so that, at the moment of death, he did not forget God. Mary had also shielded his soul so that no demons could attack him. When the verdict of Charles' soul was delivered, Mary was there defending him; how this happened she was going to tell Bridget some days later.[24]

Controversy between Mary, the angel and the devil

Virgin Mary kept her promise. Some days later, when Bridget was lost in prayer, she received a long revelation. She saw everything as Mary had described it in a long vision "through distance of time and in a physical metaphor so that your common sense can understand it", the struggle

---

[23]   Book 7, Chapter 14.

[24]   Book 7, Chapter 13.

between the devil on one side and the Virgin Mary and the angel on the other to seize Charles' soul.

Jesus is sitting on the throne with Mary by his side. In front of them, there is a frightened and naked soul (Charles). On his right and left sides, separate from him, there are an angel and a devil. The devil is complaining to Jesus that Mary has wrongfully seized Charles. As he was a sinner, he should be given to the devil. Mary answered that his soul loved God's Mother very much and thus he also learnt to love her Son. That is the reason why she takes care of him. The devil argues that he in any case wants to seize Charles, considering God's fairness: he knows all his sins. But as he is going to recite the details of them, he discovers that his memory has been erased. The angel declares that this has happened thanks to Mary's intercessions and as God's Son gave Charles this favour: for each of his sins he felt remorse, so that he submissively confessed his love for God. Therefore these sins have been forgotten. The devil exclaims: "My power has been taken away from me! The sack that was full with sins is not only empty, but has also been taken away from me! In this sack I had put all my reasons to punish him for his laziness, and because of his laziness, he neglected to do many good things."[25]

The devil does not give up yet. He asks to be able to punish Charles for his lack of good actions and virtues. But the angel answers that thanks to Charles' burning longing to go on a pilgrimage to the Holy Land, he obtained a treasure in heaven. The devil makes a last, desperate effort, asking to adjust Charles' crown so that it becomes incomplete. But to this the angel answers that whoever has been saved from hell shall receive God's grace and that God is happy to give them the crown. "For that reason, have you, devil, no right to do anything with his crown." And the devil vanished.

All these revelations, in which Bridget learnt about her son Charles, were full of consolation for her. At the same time, she had the benefit of learning about divine fairness.[26]

---

[25]   Book 7, Chapter 13.

[26]   Book 7, Chapter 13.

Golgotha and the vision of Jesus' crucifixion

On the right side of the entrance to the church, there is a steep staircase leading up to the hill called Golgotha or Mount Calvary. The first thing we see there is a beautiful mosaic in a neo-Gothic style, the gift of the Italian state at the beginning of the 1930s. It shows Station XI, the place where Jesus was nailed to the cross. On the left side, we find the altar built on the place where Jesus' cross was erected, Station XII.

Between these two stations there is a bust of Mary in a glass-setting, representing Stabat Mater, Jesus' mother standing under the cross, created to represent Mary's suffering during the crucifixion of her son.

What is left of the rock is mostly enclosed, but below the altar there is a cavity, in which the cross was placed. On the right and left sides of the altar and below the glass plate, parts of the rock can still be seen. A great part of it is also visible from Adam's chapel, situated below the altar of the crucifixion. Here, under a glass pane, there is a crevice in the rock. According to tradition, it was formed during the earthquake that began when Jesus was still on the cross. In the crevice there is a stone, whose shape reminds us of a skull. Tradition has named it "Adam's skull".

Here, at the altar of the crucifixion, the promise of coming to the Lamb came true to Bridget. When praying at the place where Jesus was crucified, she was enraptured and received something more than a revelation. She was taken 13 centuries back in time and saw the passion and crucifixion taking place in front of her. She saw Jesus being mocked, whipped and hung on the cross. She saw the soldiers putting him to scorn and the women in despair. She saw how Jesus stopped breathing and died, how he was taken down from the cross and put in Mary's arms.[27] The vision was completed by the revelation in which Virgin Mary describes the drama around her Son's crucifixion, and explains her feelings in detail.[28]

---

[27] Book 7, Chapter 15.

[28] Book 4, Chapter 70.

Bridget's revelations, authentic and down to earth

When we attempt to discern how credible Bridget's revelations are, we find a very interesting detail. Describing Jesus' crucifixion, she says that "His hand was pierced with a nail, where the bone was firmest. Then, with a rope they took out His left hand and attached it on the cross in the same way."[29] In all the representations of the crucifixion, Jesus has the palm of his hands pierced, something that was not possible, as the palms would never have borne the weight of his body. On the contrary, Bridget lets the nails pierce "the place where the bone was firmest", that is on the wrist. Scientists have later confirmed this idea.

Bridget goes on to describe how Jesus was taken down from the cross and his position in the Pietà. According to the Swedish Bridget expert Aron Andersson in his book *Bridget and the Holy Land*, Pietà images had a magnificent renaissance around the fourteenth and fifteenth centuries. At the same time, the presentation of the subject was renewed. There is every reason to believe that Bridget's revelation was the source of it. Until 1380, the dead Jesus was represented sitting on Mary's knees, later in a reclining position. According to the revelation that Bridget received in Jerusalem, Mary is resting with her right hand on Jesus' head and with the left she is touching his breast, hair, his stiff arms and his pierced hands that were lying crossed beneath his lower abdomen.

Jesus' torture and death are not only a vision: his own mother Mary gave Bridget a detailed report on how it happened. Here, in contrast to what the Gospels tell, it is a woman, a mother, telling in the first person what an indescribable pain she had to endure, while she saw her own Son's pain and death.

---

[29] Book 7, Chapter 15.

The Crypt

On the eastern side of the church, stairs lead down to a crypt dedicated to Constantine's mother Helena, who came to the Holy Land with her son in 324. The sides of the staircase are covered with crosses carved by the Crusaders. The crypt has three naves with a cupola built during the twelfth century, when the present church was built. From the crypt it is possible to enter two smaller chapels. The one on the right, some steps down, is said to be the place where Helena found the true cross.

The chapel on the left, named after St Vartan, contains one of the testimonies of the first Christian pilgrims: a marble slab that was originally placed in the temple that Emperor Hadrian had built in AD 135. On it, there is a boat with the inscription: *Domine ivimus*: Lord, we are coming! The inscription is dated between 135 and 330 and is certainly the first witness by Christian pilgrims visiting the place. The text describes a successful boat trip and how thankful the pilgrims were to have reached the Church of the Holy Sepulchre. When Bridget read it, it must have struck a chord for her, remembering the dramatic boat trip she had had before reaching Jerusalem.

The Chapel of the Derision

Leaving the crypt, on the left side of the stairs, there is the Chapel of the Derision, where a big fragment of a column is venerated. According to popular belief, it is part of a column in Pilate's palace in Jerusalem, to which Jesus was tied when he was scourged. The other part of it is said to be in Rome. But as this column is very different from the one in Rome—it is thicker, darker and of another kind of stone—its authenticity has been questioned. The two very different pieces cannot have come from the same column; at least one of them is false, maybe both are. In spite of this, Bridget has prayed at both and thus classified them as authentic. How can that be?

How could Bridget declare this inconsequential? In the book *The Return of St. Bridget*, the author allows Bridget to express her opinion. He imagines that she has come back from praying at the stone as she had done several times in Jerusalem and is now pondering Christ's suffering when he was tied to the column. When the author has told her what he is thinking, Bridget comes with the following explanation:

> I am not going to blame you, I too had similar ideas when I lived in Rome. The worst of all was when I visited St Peter's Church on a Good Friday, when Veronica's holy shroud was shown to the public. I was in the company of an ungodly knight from Sweden. But instead of being converted, he started putting the believers to scorn for their faith and making fun of the shroud that according to him was not authentic. I must confess, that I, too, started doubting its authenticity. But then God's Son appeared and gave me a word on the road: "What My shroud becomes, as the bloody sweat came out of My body, when I before My Passion had prayed to God, in the same way, the same sweat came down from my face for her who prayed to me and for a consolation for later generations."[30]
>
> It is not so much question about the authenticity of the shroud or the column, but that our Lord has really been scourged at a column and that He had His bloody face cleaned by the merciful Veronica. We cannot prove the authenticity of the objects, but we know that they are here for the consolation of later generations.

The Blessed Virgin Mary as a witness to the resurrection

Constantine's round church, called the Anastasia Rotunda, was built over the tomb of Jesus, which is in the centre of the church. The tomb consists of a small chapel with a suite of two rooms. The first one is called the Chapel of the Angel. It contains the stone on which the angel had been sitting when the women entered the empty tomb. The other one is the Tomb Chambre, identical with Station XIV and the last one on Via Dolorosa, but also the one that in the promises is called The Snake. The

---

[30] Book 4, Chapter 81.

very place Jesus was present is covered by a smooth and now worn marble slab, which has been there since 1555.

The wall of the Anastasia Rotunda opens to a set of lateral aisles which are all connected with Jesus' suffering, death and resurrection. One seems to be identical with the new tomb that Joseph of Arimathea bought after having given his first one to Jesus. A smaller chapel was built during the ninth century and consecrated to the memory of Jesus' first resurrection appearance to his mother.

Death was not the end; Jesus rose from the dead on Easter Day. This is not only confirmed by the empty tomb, but also by many eyewitnesses. One of these is Jesus' own mother. It is with great joy that the Virgin Mary leaves a description of the victory over death, when her Son, as she expresses it, strong as a lion, routed the devil's power and liberated the souls in the kingdom of the dead. Mary tells Bridget that she was the first one who witnessed the resurrection but remained silent about it then. It is almost possible to believe that the Gospels and the revelation are opposed to each other. But if we take a closer look at the Gospels, it is never said there that Mary Magdalene was the first one at the tomb, but only that she went to it. About the Virgin Mary nothing is said. The reason is, as she explained it in the revelation, that from pure humility she wanted Mary Magdalene to take the credit for it, something she also did.[31]

The dubbing of Birger

In the revelation above (Book 7, Chapter 13), there is mention of Charles becoming a knight as Mary had given him spiritual weapons and clothes to be used by knights when they enter heaven to approach God. The idea was that both brothers, Charles and Birger, should come with their mother to Jerusalem and be made Knights of the Holy Sepulchre. Only Birger was now to be knighted during a solemn ceremony. It took place in the Holy Sepulchre, where Birger had to take the oath:

---

[31]   Book 6, Chapter 94.

> I, Birger Ulfsson, promise God and you, venerable Father, to
> defend the holy church against its enemies, to protect God's
> friends, to take care of widows and fatherless children, and if I
> make mistakes in some action, I will submit to your punishment,
> so that I will fully comply with God's and your wish.

After he said these words, the priest put the robe of the order on him
as a sign that he now had a superior to obey. And when he received his
sword in his hand, the priest said: "With this sword you shall fight against
God's enemies." When he received the shield, he said: "This shield shall
save you against the enemies' arrows. This shield shall rather break than
you should flee."

It must have been a very precious moment for Bridget, as she, as a
mother, must have felt an indescribable pride in a double sense; one of
her sons had his soul saved, the other one was created a knight!

The Knights of the Holy Sepulchre

The order of the Knights of the Holy Sepulchre of Jerusalem dates back
to the beginning of the twelfth century. It still exists and is active today.
Its Latin name is: *Ordo Equestris Sancti Sepulcri Hierosolymitani.* It is
an official Roman Catholic order of knights under the jurisdiction of the
pope. It describes its purpose as follows:

> In fidelity to the Pope and the Catholic Church, it shall teach and
> strengthen the members' spiritual life and their will to assist in
> different ways the Holy Land, support and help with merciful,
> social and cultural work in the Holy Land, especially the work
> done by the Latin (catholic) patriarchate of Jerusalem, assemble
> the Catholics of the world and other brothers and sisters in Christ
> in order to preserve and strengthen the faith in the Holy Land
> as well as to keep the privileges of the Catholic Church in the
> Holy Land.

The order also aims, through spiritual and economic help, to prevent holy places from becoming merely museums and tourist sites. A very important task for the Knights of the Holy Sepulchre is to promote peace between Christians, Jews and Muslims living in the Holy Land. In spite of the fact that the investiture follows today the same ritual as took place during Bridget's days, their tasks are only peaceful, social and humanitarian. Today's knights promote medical and social help on a Catholic basis, and those who are made knights or ladies of the Holy Sepulchre have to promise a lifelong commitment to Jerusalem and the Holy Land.

As papal knights, the order has a cardinal as its Grand Master. The knights and the ladies, in all around 22,000 members, have the pope's assignment to act as the Latin patriarch's economic backbone.

1 0

In and around Jerusalem

Via Dolorosa in reverse direction

According to the accounts of pilgrims from the Middle Ages, Jerusalem had a guided route through the city on which the pilgrims could visit in one day the most important holy places. Guided by Franciscan cicerones, the tour took them along the Via Dolorosa, but in the reverse direction. Via Dolorosa in Latin means "Way of Suffering". Along it a pilgrim route covers the way Jesus went when carrying his cross from his death sentence in the Antonia Fortress, close to the Sheep Gate, up to Golgotha, the place of the crucifixion. As early as Byzantine times, Christian pilgrims walked along this road, but it had a real revival during the period after 1350 when the Franciscan friars were chosen by the pope to be the keepers of the holy places. The road is about 600 metres in length and winds like a staircase through the old town. There are 14 Stations of the Cross, of which the last five are in the Church of the Holy Sepulchre. The traditions of the Via Dolorosa are partly based on the accounts of the New Testament Gospels and partly on later Christian tradition.

The pilgrims gathered early in the morning outside the Church of the Holy Sepulchre. Then, by the light of their torches, they walked along the narrow streets to Station IX. It was marked with a column, built inside on the left side of the entrance to the Coptic Church, marking the place where Jesus fell for the third time. A little further on, on the wall of a Greek monastery, there is a stone with a Latin cross and an inscription in Greek saying: "Jesus has conquered". This is Station VIII. In the corner, where the Via Dolorosa turns to the right, pilgrims arrive at Station VII, the place where Jesus fell for the second time. It is believed that here was the "Door of the Judgement", where the names of the convicted were displayed. It is also the door through which he left the town on his way to his crucifixion. A little further away is Station VI, where according to tradition, Veronica's home was situated. Veronica is the woman who is said to have wiped Jesus' face with a shroud. The shroud, according to tradition, is now kept in St Peter's Basilica in Rome. When she saw the house, Bridget must have thought of the dispute she had had about the shroud with a Swedish earl in the church, when the shroud was shown to the public one Good Friday.

There was a longer stop at Station V, at the church belonging to the Franciscans. It marks the place where Simon of Cyrene took the cross from Jesus. During the Middle Ages, it was thought that the place was also the home of Lazarus, the main character in the parable of "the rich man and Lazarus". Although we know that a parable is a story with a heavenly meaning and does not depict a real event, it was nevertheless a parable of great importance to the Franciscans, whose concern for the poor identified with the story of poor Lazarus. He was afforded consolation in his pain, but it also showed the consequences of not following one's proper social responsibilities (Luke 16:19–31).

Where the road turns to the left, the group arrived at Station IV, where Mary met her son carrying his cross. Further ahead on the right, at the intersection, is Station III, the place where Jesus fell for the first time. Not far from there is an arch over the Via Dolorosa. On the left side, there are two big stones, one of which is said to have been in Pontius Pilate's palace, where Jesus stood. On the other one Pontius Pilate showed the bloody and lacerated Jesus to the people, saying, *Ecce Homo*, Behold the Man!

After the arch is Station II. Here in the Franciscan chapel is the place where Jesus was flogged and had the cross put onto his back. The pilgrims with Bridget were not allowed to enter the chapel, as it was occupied by some Muslim families. They had therefore to pray outside. A few metres further away, on the other side of the road, there is a yard today belonging to a Muslim school. This is Station I. It was exactly here, inside the *praetorium*, that Jesus was interrogated and sentenced to death. This is the end of the pilgrims' way along the Via Dolorosa, but certainly not the end of the pilgrims' visit to the places of the Holy Land.

The home of the Virgin Mary's parents

On the other side is St Anne's Church, which, according to church tradition, was the home of Joachim and Anne, the parents of the Virgin Mary. A church was built on this place as early as the fifth century. It was later replaced by the Crusaders in 1142 with a magnificent Gothic church, established by Queen Arda of Armenia, the widow of King Baldwin I of Jerusalem. She later retired to a convent not far from the church.

When Salah ad-Din (1138–93) conquered Jerusalem in 1187, the church was transformed into a mosque and the convent into a *madrassa*. During the Ottoman period, the whole building was left to fall into decay, and it was not until the middle of the nineteenth century that the building could be used as a church again, after the French order of the White Fathers took over the trusteeship.

The Crusaders stated that Mary had been born in a cave, which could be reached through a staircase inside the church. But when Bridget arrived, it was forbidden for Christians to use the staircase, as the church had been converted into a mosque. It was nevertheless possible to reach the cave by being lowered from a low window, which is still there, but only after giving extra money to the guards. Mary's place of birth was important for Bridget. It is on that place that Mary's promise to Bridget to become a vessel for Mary's glory will be fulfilled. Mary was saying that as a vessel for God she was not clean, as she was descended from Adam and born from sinners, but yet she was clean as she was conceived without sin, so that the Son too should be born without sin. For that reason, Mary ends, "whoever comes to this place, where Mary was born and raised, shall not only be clean but also a vessel for my glory".[32]

There is no doubt that Mary's parents Joachim and Anne were also remembered, as during the Middle Ages they had been objects of great devotion. Earlier, in Rome, Bridget had revelations in which Joachim and Anne were shown as a model married couple.[33] In another revelation,

---

[32]   Book 5, Chapter 13.
[33]   Book 6, Chapter 104.

Mary emphasizes Joachim and Anne's importance as parents of the Virgin Mary, who was to be the Saviour's mother.[34]

In the garden around the church is the Pool of Bethesda, which had been uncovered by archaeologists. It is situated at 13 metres below the present ground level. During the Middle Ages it was possible to descend a very steep staircase in order to see and feel the wonder-working water in a dark hole below the ground.

We associate the pool mainly with Jesus' healing of a man who had been paralysed for 38 years. It happened on a Sabbath, the Jewish day of rest, and the Gospel tells us that the man, who could now walk, reached the temple which was situated close by (John 5:1–15). But our pilgrims were unable to access it. The old temple site, where the Dome of the Rock and the Al Aqsa Mosque were situated, is considered one of Islam's most holy places. Christians were strictly forbidden to enter. If anyone tried and was caught, they were given two choices: they had to renounce their Christian faith and convert to Islam or be sawn in two while still alive!

The Golden Gate

Bridget's pilgrims continued east through the Sheep Gate, or as it is now called Stephen's or the Lion Gate. They could then make a detour on the right in order to see the so-called Golden Gate, known as the place where Jesus made his triumphant entrance to the city on Palm Sunday. It was the closest they could get to the temple. According to pilgrims' reports from the fourteenth century, ever since Jesus entered the Gate on his donkey, it has not been possible to open it again. But this is not correct. When Jerusalem was still in the hands of the Crusaders, it was opened every Palm Sunday. But when Bridget arrived, two centuries had already passed and the Gate was permanently closed. According to Jewish tradition, the Messiah will enter this Gate. For that reason, the Ottoman sultan Suleiman I had the Gate closed in 1541 in order to prevent the Messiah from entering. To be on the safe side, he also had a Muslim cemetery built in front of it.

---

[34]   Book 6, Chapter 55.

The place of St Stephen's execution

After this detour, the pilgrims continued towards the Mount of Olives until they reached the place outside the Sheep Gate, where St Stephen was stoned to death (Acts 6–7). He became the first Christian martyr. His stoning took place on a slanting rock with low steps in the direction of Jerusalem. One hundred years ago, the rock, still in good condition, was covered by a chapel belonging to the Greek Orthodox Church.

Stephen's promise to Bridget that she would see the place where he had suffered a martyr's death was now fulfilled. In a revelation, which Bridget received in Rome, Stephen told her in detail about his mission, in which he participated together with the apostles in order to do what had been entrusted to him. He also told her about the three things which helped him to endure the martyrdom: the apostles' prayers and Jesus' suffering and love.[35]

The apostle Paul's description of his eyewitness account of Stephen's martyrdom is very moving. It is reported in a revelation that Bridget received in Rome in the Church of St Paul Outside the Walls, many years earlier. Paul had held the coats of the people who had stoned Stephen, as he was sure this was the right thing to do. But, according to him, he felt uneasy about what was happening. In some way Paul felt a compassion for Stephen, praying that his suffering could bring him honour and compensation. In that way, Paul was one of the first who, to use his own words: "through Stephen's intercession was taken away from the wolves and became a mild lamb". At the end of the revelation Paul says: "the prayers of the just ones will help those who are closest to mercy".[36]

The empty tomb of the Virgin Mary

The road from the Sheep Gate to the Mount of Olives winds through the Kidron valley, over the creek Kidron that is difficult to see, to the place where, according to legend, the wood for the cross of Jesus was collected.

---

[35]   Book 6, Chapter 108.
[36]   Book 6, Chapter 108.

At the foot of the Mount of Olives, in the valley on the other side of the creek, was the Church of the Tomb of the Virgin Mary. The church, known since the fifth century, was destroyed by Sultan Al Hakim in 1009, but rebuilt by the Crusaders around 1130. A Benedictine monastery was then established by monks from Cluny. After the Crusaders' defeat, negotiations took place during 1333–5 between the sultan of Egypt En-Naser Mohammed and the royal couple of Naples Sanchez and Robert Anjou to allow the Franciscans to manage the church. Negotiations broke down because of the brief Crusader raid against Alexandria by King Peter I of Cyprus in 1365, but through an intermediary from Queen Johanna of Naples, in the late fourteenth century the Franciscans obtained the right to administer the Chapel of the Tomb and its altar. Since 1767, the church has been owned by the Armenian and Greek Orthodox churches.

From the porch with its low, pointed Gothic arch, there is a steep staircase of 48 steps, lit by burning candles and leading down to the lower floor area. Halfway, on the right side, is Queen Melisenda's tomb (1105–61). She was the wife of Fulk (1089–1143), count of Anjou and the king of Jerusalem. The chapel is also dedicated to Mary's parents, Joachim and Anne. Opposite, on the left side, is the crypt housing the tomb of Queen Bodil Thrugotsdatter (1056–1103), wife of King Erik the Good of Denmark, who died in Paphos before reaching the Holy Land. This chapel has also been devoted to Joseph, Mary's husband and Jesus' foster father. The church has the shape of a Latin cross. The Virgin Mary's tomb, carved into the rock, can be seen in the eastern transept.

During Bridget's visit, an agreement was in place that, if pilgrims wanted to celebrate Mass, they had to do it before sunrise, since every day Muslim worshippers came to the tomb to pray; they also wanted to pay their respect to "Merja", Jesus' mother, of whom they thought highly. Today, part of this agreement can still be seen on the right side of the tomb, in a "Mihrab" niche. Even today, Muslims come here to pray. Like many Christians, they also believe that Jesus was born of a virgin, though they do not consider Jesus to be God's Son, but one of the greatest prophets, and for that reason Jesus' mother Merja receives their veneration. The Muslims still believe, and in this they differ from Christian belief, that Mary, or Merja, is still in the tomb.

Bridget shared the Christian belief that Mary, after her death, was bodily assumed into heaven. This is clearly confirmed by some of Mary's revelations. In one of them she asserts that, deplorably, there are still some Christians who do not share this belief. The Virgin Mary disassociates herself strongly from the belief which some people had "who did not know better" leaving a very detailed description of the course of events.[37]

In all the revelations regarding this matter, the Virgin Mary relates what happened to her after her Son's ascension. She lived over 15 years after that. The Christian tradition specifies 15 August as the day of the Dormition of Mary. She was later put in the tomb, according to what Mary revealed, where she stayed for only 15 days before being taken to heaven. No details are left out: Mary is very careful when it comes to describing that her old robes were left in the tomb while she was clothed with the same robes as her Son. And in order to avoid misunderstandings, something that was very common also during Bridget's days, Mary clarifies that in heaven there are only two human bodies: her own and that of her Son.[38]

Not so far from this place, at the foot of the Mount of Olives, the Bridgettine Sisters opened a guesthouse with 15 rooms and in all 33 sleeping accommodations in 2006, called the John Paul II Center for Interreligious Dialogue.

The cave and garden of Gethsemane

On the right side of the front of Mary's church, there is the Gethsemane Cave, today converted into a chapel, where Jesus went with his apostles to pray. On the left side of the altar, there is the stone on which Jesus had knelt at his third prayer during the dramatic night before he was captured. On the wall above it there is an inscription in Latin from the first part of the fourteenth century engraved by the Franciscans saying: "Here the Holy King sweated blood when He was praying: 'Father, if you

---

[37] Book 1, Chapter 9.

[38] Book 6, Chapter 62.

are willing, please take this cup of suffering away from me. Yet I want your will to be done, not mine."

On the other side of the Hosanna Road, there is the Garden of Gethsemane, today covered with olive trees as in Bridget's days. The extremely old trees, even if not the same as during Jesus' days, derive from those which witnessed the dramatic hours during which Jesus' agony and arrest took place. When Bridget passed here with her company, she could still see the Crusaders' Church from the twelfth century, which had been abandoned in 1345. It was built on the ruins of an earlier Byzantine basilica. Today, on the same place, there is a majestic church built by the Franciscan friars in 1924 and dedicated to "All Nations".

The girdle of the Virgin Mary

The pilgrim path continues on the steep road up to the Mount of Olives. It is not clear whether Bridget undertook the entire pilgrimage route in one day or if she had to split it into different stages for her age and health's sake. In any case, she had another important destination to visit: the place of Jesus' ascension. On their way to it, the pilgrims took the opportunity to visit some other holy sites. Then the Franciscan guides stopped at the place of Mary's assumption into heaven which, according to the apocryphal Gospels and ancient Christian tradition, was witnessed by the apostle Thomas. When Thomas visited Mary's empty tomb, he had doubts about her ascension, but then Mary showed herself to the sceptical apostle and as a sign she took off her belt and let it fall into his hands. This relic, a knitted girdle in green yarn with golden embroidery, is now kept in the Cathedral of Prato north of Florence.

Dominus Flevit and Eleona

The next stop was at Dominus Flevit, a little chapel built on the site where Jesus cried over Jerusalem. At that time, the church was in ruins, but in 1955 a new church was built and shaped like a tear.

On their way, the pilgrims passed the ruins of the Eleona basilica, the foremost building that Mother Empress Helen had built in memory of Jesus' ascension. It was completed in 333, an enormous church with an atrium, a garden and a crypt. The basilica was not located exactly where the ascension took place, but was nearby. It was from here that the annual procession on Palm Sunday to Jerusalem began.

The basilica was first destroyed by the Persians in 614 and again in 1009 by the notorious caliph Al-Hakim. Since then, Eleona has been left a ruin. The Palm Sunday procession still takes place, but now from the Pater Noster Church.

The Pater Noster Cave

The Pater Noster Church was also a ruin during the fourteenth century, but the cave from where Jesus is said to have taught his disciples the Lord's Prayer is still there. During the Middle Ages it was thought that it was here that the apostles met in order to compile the Apostolic Creed, but it is known now that it was formulated much later, i.e. about AD 150. The cave is now a crypt in the Carmelite church that was built in 1874. In the convent garden, the walls are covered by glazed tiles on which it is possible to read the Lord's Prayer in many different languages, including Braille.

The Chapel of the Ascension

Finally, at the top of the Mount of Olives, 812 metres above sea level, the pilgrims reached the site that, according to the promise Bridget received, was represented by an eagle. It was here that, in 370, a noble Roman lady ordered an octagonal church to be built, which in size and shape can be seen as a prototype of the Dome of the Rock that was built three centuries later on the remnants of the Temple of Jerusalem. In 614, the church was destroyed by the Persians, but later rebuilt by the Crusaders. In 1187, it was transformed into a mosque after Saladin won back Jerusalem. Like Christians, Muslims also believe in Jesus' ascension.

From Bridget's days, we have a very detailed description of the shrine. A broad staircase in front of the loggia took you into the chapel; it is described as round, but actually it is octagonal with a large, beautiful round opening in the middle of the roof. Inside the church, there were beautiful marble columns, paintings and sculptures. Today, nothing of these remain but, in the middle of the chapel, there is a marble slab on which, according to tradition, Jesus left his footprints. At the entrance, the pilgrims had to pay half a dirhem per person. Today the Chapel of the Ascension is still managed by Muslims and pilgrims are required to pay a small entrance fee. Nowadays, the place is regarded as holy by both Christians and Muslims, and the Franciscans are permitted to celebrate Mass inside the chapel on Ascension Day.

The leadership of the Church

It is from this place that Jesus, 40 days after the resurrection, ascended to heaven. After he had left them, his disciples had to wait for the sending of the Holy Spirit before they could go out and bring the good news to all the people of the world. But there were still ten days before Pentecost and who would fill the vacuum now, when Jesus had gone? Yes, the person who was closest to him, that is the Virgin Mary. This is what an angel had disclosed to Bridget already during her first time in Rome, when she was writing down the so-called *Sermo Angelicus*: the Angel's dictation, the morning prayer or Matins, that was later used by the Bridgettine nuns of Vadstena.

In a revelation, an angel disclosed to Bridget how Mary, dedicated and focused, took over the direction of the Church. The angel enumerated all her tasks, which among others dealt with strengthening the good people, reprimanding those who went astray, teaching the believers by giving them her help, and strengthening the martyrs.

Further, she would exhort married couples, comfort the widows and be an example to those who were virgins. She was also practical in instructing people to have the right balance of sleep, food and work. And in her role as a *locum tenens* she guided the apostles, even telling or explaining to them things previously hidden from them about her Son and his doctrine.[39]

The Pool of Siloam

The pilgrims left the Chapel of the Ascension and retraced their steps in the direction of Gethsemane. After crossing the Kidron creek they turned to the left, passing what was thought to be the tombs of Absalom and Zechariah. It had been a mortuary monument since Jesus' days, one of the few remaining of his time. By following the Kidron valley on the slope below the town wall to the south it was possible to reach the Pool of Siloam.

An underpass, built by King Hezekiah around the year 700 BC, discharged its water into the pool. The water, which came from the Gihon spring, also called the Mary spring outside the town walls on the left side of the Kidron valley, was directed to Jerusalem in order to help the people in the event of a siege. The pool is mentioned in John 9:1–11, the story of the man born blind whose sight was restored by Jesus.

Originally the pool was surrounded by a majestic colonnade. What we see today is what was rebuilt during the sixth century. When Bridget visited it, the water was not fit to drink as it was used by the Saracens to tan leather.

Gallicantu

On the other side of the road, on the slope of Mount Zion, there are the remains of a wide stone staircase. There is no doubt that it was there also before Jesus' day, and it is possible that he used it with his disciples. According to tradition, it was the site of the High Priest's palace and garden, where Peter denied his Master three times before he heard the cock crow, as Jesus had foretold (Luke 22:34): "Jesus answered, 'I tell

---

[39]   *Sermo Angelicus.* Saturday's first reading.

you, Peter, before the rooster crows today, you will deny three times that you know me.'"

For that reason, the place is called Gallicantu, which means "the cock crowed". During Bridget's days, it was still possible to see the remains of an old church built in 457 in the Byzantine style; it was destroyed in 1010 by Al-Hakim. In 1102, it was rebuilt, but was destroyed again in later years. A new church was eventually built in 1931. Below the church, one can see what is thought was the High Priest's prison in his palace.

Mount Zion

The pilgrims' next focus was another hill with numerous shrines: Mount Zion, situated south-west just beyond the wall of the old city. Here was the place where the Virgin Mary spent her last seven years and where she died. There were also the ruins of the church where the apostle John said Mass for the Virgin Mary, where Matthias was chosen as an apostle and James the Less was appointed bishop of Jerusalem. Here is also the room where Jesus established the Eucharist, where he appeared after the resurrection and where the Holy Spirit was poured out at Pentecost.

Mount Zion was the home of the first Christian community and the oldest episcopal see. A large basilica was erected here during the fourth century. It was destroyed 600 years later, was rebuilt by the Crusaders only to be torn to pieces in 1219 by the Egyptian sultan Malik Al Kamil (1180–1238) as he had destroyed many of the churches built by the Crusaders. It seems that the only room to escape destruction was where Jesus established the Eucharist. Also the Byzantine Hagia Maria (or Dormition) Abbey on Mount Zion—which tradition states was the place where the Virgin Mary died—was destroyed in the same year and was only a ruin when Bridget visited. The church we see today was built at the beginning of the twentieth century at the request of Wilhelm II, then emperor of Germany. In spite of his Protestant faith, he wanted to be an emperor for both Catholics and Protestants. He donated the church to the "Union of German Catholics of the Holy Land".

A tradition from the fifth century says that the apostle John took care of Jesus' mother at his home on Zion. Another tradition asserts that he took her to Ephesus. It is difficult to establish which version is correct, but according to the tradition in Jerusalem, almost all the disciples were assembled there when Mary died, except for James, who had suffered martyrdom, and Thomas, who had undertaken to spread the gospel message to India. According to tradition, when Thomas came back, he wanted to see Mary's body, but found the tomb empty and heard the sound of celestial songs being sung. But as he was doubtful about Mary's ascension, Jesus' mother showed herself to Thomas on the Mount of Olives.

At the beginning of the fourteenth century, the whole area was bought by the king and the queen of Sicily for 32,000 ducats. It was later given to the pope on the condition that the Franciscan friars should be its guardians for an indeterminable period. The office of Custodia Terrae Sanctae was established in a bull by Clement VI dated 21 November 1342. The Franciscans were also given the task of restoring the upper room, which is why it has a Gothic structure with pointed arches.

When Bridget was there, she must have remembered the revelation she had during Pentecost, when she still lived in Alvastra. Then Jesus had explained to her why the Holy Spirit should come:

> He came to the disciples in a threefold way: as a stream to fill their joints and limbs with a divine complacency and solace. He came as a fire for the divine ardour of love and lighted so their hearts so they did not love and dread anything but God. He came as tongues, and as the tongues are inside the mouth but do not hurt the mouth but, on the contrary, help it to speak, the Holy Spirit was in their souls and did not let them yearn for anything but Him and helped them speak with divine wisdom.[40]

According to tradition, David, Solomon and other kings were buried below the sanctuary in Zion. In 1523, in an order from Sultan Suleiman I (1495–1566), the Franciscans were evicted from the convent and the upper room was transformed into a mosque. For a long period, Christians

---

[40] Book 6, Chapter 36.

were not allowed to enter and traces of the Islamic decoration from that time can still be found on the site.

Since the founding of the state of Israel in 1948, the site has a neutral status and is used as a museum, and neither Christians nor Muslims are permitted to use it as a place of worship. An exception was made for the visit of Pope Francis in May 2014. The pope was able to celebrate a solemn pontifical High Mass in the place where the Eucharist is said to have been instituted. This caused a strong reaction from ultra-Orthodox Jews who, a few days later, stormed the hall and drove away the Christian pilgrims who were there. One of the banners used at the protest read: "Pope stay in Rome. King David's tomb belongs to the Jewish people!"

The Cathedral of St James

The way back to the Holy Sepulchre went through the Jaffa Gate. It was rebuilt in 1436 along with the restructuring of the walls during the Turkish epoch. Inside the walls, our pilgrims could visit one of the most impressive and beautiful cathedrals in Jerusalem. It is situated in what is the Armenian quarter in the old city. The church, dedicated to the apostle James the Great, was built during the twelfth century and rebuilt again 100 years later. It was here, according to church tradition, that the apostle James, later bishop of Jerusalem, was beheaded in AD 44 by order of Herod Agrippa, who governed Judea from AD 41 until his death in AD 44. In the western aisle of the church, the place of his execution is marked, and there his head was venerated. No doubt that Bridget knelt at the stone, while remembering her pilgrimage to Santiago with her husband Ulf in 1341–2. Inside the church there were stones from holy places in the Holy Land: Sinai, Tabor and Jordan. They have been placed there for people who for economic or health reasons cannot go on a pilgrimage to those places. Here, the "places" come to the pilgrims.

The Tower of David

After having left the Armenian quarter, the group passed, on the left side of the citadel, the so-called David's Tower, which was and still is an important fortress. It is an area with the three towers that Herod the Great (73–7 BC) built in 37–34 BC to defend his palace nearby. It was there that Herod received the wise men when they were searching for the newly born Messiah (Matthew 2:1–12). The citadel was saved during the Roman Emperor Titus' siege to give shelter to his twelfth legion. During the Byzantine period, the place was a heap of ruins, but the pilgrims always stopped there to pray and meditate. The Crusaders rebuilt the fortress during the 1100s, but it was destroyed once more in 1239, this time by the Mamluks, so it was a ruin even when our pilgrims visited the city. The citadel was then rebuilt by the Turks in 1541 and remained intact. Today, it houses a museum about the history of the country.

Late in the afternoon, the group ended their tour at the Holy Sepulchre. This was the classic route taken by pilgrims during the Middle Ages. It was calculated that the tour should take almost 24 hours. It is obvious that there would be detours, or the tour could be followed in the opposite direction. We can suppose that Bridget completed the tour on several days during her four-months-long stay in the Holy Land, and that she often returned to places she liked best.

There were also many more important destinations for her outside the Holy City.

To the River Jordan

Most pilgrimages to the Holy Land include a visit to the River Jordan; some also visit the Dead Sea. For the pilgrims of Bridget's day, this was a major trip. It took several days and included several visits to places connected with stories in the Bible.

The old pilgrim road from Jerusalem down to the River Jordan is around 40 kilometres long, meandering from the Mount of Olives through Bethphage, Bethany and Jericho. It is the same route that Jesus followed on his last journey to Jerusalem. Now Bridget and her friends used the same steep road but in the opposite direction, descending 1000 metres. The road was tortuous and steep, and it was also dangerous. Bandits preyed upon pilgrims, which was why they always travelled in large groups. The trip was made more difficult by the restrictions imposed on Christians. For example, they were not allowed to use horses to ride; they could use donkeys, but only to carry luggage and supplies.

Bethphage

After one kilometre from Jerusalem, our pilgrims stopped at Bethphage to look at the stone that Jesus had stood on to mount the donkey that was to take him to Jerusalem on Palm Sunday. On the stone, that has been in the Crusaders' church since the 1100s, there is a fresco from the same period, depicting Jesus' entry into Jerusalem.

In the same place, it is said that Jesus met Martha who, in despair, told him of the death of her brother Lazarus.

Bethany

Not far from Bethphage was Bethany, where the siblings Martha, Mary and Lazarus lived. Today, the village is called Al-Eizariya, meaning Lazarus' place. The pilgrims visited Lazarus' tomb, which was, and still is, owned by the Muslims. Today one can enter it by taking 24 steep steps down, which were dug out some 400 years ago. The Church of St Lazarus was built there around 1950. This modern church includes also parts of the old churches from the fourth to the sixth and the twelfth centuries.

Two sisters in Bethany

When Bridget was in Rome, she received a long revelation about the two sisters Martha and Mary. In Luke's Gospel, Martha is described as a houseproud woman, while Mary is more contemplative. Mary preferred sitting at Jesus' feet, while Martha was working hard in the kitchen. This made Martha irritated when Jesus visited them: "Martha was distracted by her many tasks; so she came to him and asked, 'Lord, do you not care that my sister has left me to do all the work by myself? Tell her then to help me.' But the Lord answered her, 'Martha, Martha, you are worried and distracted by many things; there is need of only one thing. Mary has chosen the better part, which will not be taken away from her.'" In the revelation Bridget received, Mary and Martha's characters were both valued.[41]

Lazarus raised from the dead

In another revelation, Jesus tells Bridget about Lazarus' resurrection, giving four reasons why he woke him from death. First, because he was a friend. Second, because of his sisters' love for him. Third, because of his sister Mary's humility. And finally, because Jesus wanted to give glory to God.

---

[41]   Book 6, Chapter 65.

The raising of Lazarus is interpreted as a metaphor for people's spiritual awakening. "Thus, I raised your brother, that is, your soul that—fetid after being dead for four days—had separated itself from me by breaking my commandments, by wrong desires and delight in the sweetness of the world and of sins." According to John's Gospel, the Jews wanted to kill Lazarus, as so many people because of him started to believe in Jesus. In other words, the soul is never left in peace, not even after having obtained new life. "The Jews," Jesus says, "who wanted to kill Lazarus, are the same as those who are arguing about the virtues of life but do not keep to them. For that reason," Jesus tells Bridget, "I will protect you and keep you away from those 'Jews', so that you will not disappear from Me through their words or acts."[42]

The inn of the Good Samaritan

Halfway to Jericho, there was an Arabian lodging house called "The Samaritan" after Jesus' parable of the Good Samaritan (Luke 10:30-7), the action of which took place on this road. During the Middle Ages, as we already discovered at Station V on the Via Dolorosa, there was a tendency to relate parables to specific places.

The pilgrims stopped at the lodging house on their way back, as it took a long time to reach because of the steep road. According to the pilgrims from Bridget's time, the lodging house consisted of an inside garden, which was a place of rest for both humans and animals. Today, what are left are the ruins of an Ottoman tavern not far away, built on the ruins of the Byzantine Monastery of St Joachim.

Jericho holds a number of records: it is the oldest and lowest situated town in the world, located at 260 metres below sea level. Ruins as old as 8,000 years have been found there. It was the walls of Jericho which collapsed when the Israelites conquered the town around 1250 BC. It was here that Jesus stopped on his way to Jerusalem to cure the blind Bartimaeus outside the town gate (Mark 10:46-52). Here, in the flowering desert, where date palms, sugar canes and every kind of fruit

---

42   Book 4, Chapter 72.

were grown, the pilgrims could break a palm leaf and take it away with them as a souvenir of the Holy Land. For that reason, Jericho was also called the city of palm trees. The most important thing to see then, and is still today, was the sycamore or mulberry tree, into which Zacchaeus climbed up, so that he would be able to see Jesus (Luke 19:1–4). Jericho, with its 20,000 inhabitants, has been administered since 1995 by the Palestinian authorities.

The River Jordan

Leaving Jericho, the pilgrims continued another ten kilometres through a desert-like mountainous landscape before they reached the River Jordan, where John the Baptist preached and where Jesus was baptized. It is situated at Mukhadat Halja, close to the John the Baptist convent. There some Greek-Orthodox monks showed them John the Baptist's dried-up hand. Sources relate that the pilgrims often went bathing in the river and those who could swim crossed to the other side of it. Afterwards an antiphonal Te Deum was sung from both sides of the river, an inspiring experience for the pilgrims.

The place is still a well-frequented pilgrim destination. Today there are staircases for the tourists leading them down in the water, a big car park, and, of course, a souvenir shop.

As early as 1350, Bridget had a revelation in Rome about this place. It was St John who told her how God and the Holy Spirit revealed themselves at Jesus' baptism and that he himself was a witness of what happened. For that reason, St John, he told her, invites everyone, rich or poor, to believe in Jesus and to walk in his way. He forestalled questions concerning Jesus' words about the camel and the eye of a needle, making it clear that rich people can reach heaven "as long as they are not tied to their richness, bestow care upon their neighbours and with all their assiduity keep watch that God is loved".[43]

---

43   Book 3, Chapter 11.

To Bethlehem

The town

Bethlehem is the small town in Judea that the prophet Micah foretold would be the birthplace of the Messiah (Micah 5:2). As it is so close to Jerusalem, it has had a troubled history and, like many more towns in Judea, it has been conquered and destroyed many times.

The distance to Bethlehem from Jerusalem is only nine kilometres, but for some reason it took Bridget and her party some time to reach it. We do not know if someone was ill, or if she wanted to leave the best destination to the last. However, in the middle of August, the group reached a Bethlehem in ruins. During the conquest of the town, the whole defensive wall was dismantled and was only rebuilt 200 years later at the time of the Ottoman Empire.

In 1967 Bethlehem, previously governed by Jordan, was occupied by Israel, and in 1994 administrative control was handed over to the Palestinian authorities. The majority of Bethlehem's 20,000 inhabitants are Muslims, but there is also a sizeable Christian population. Tourism is the main source of income for many of the residents. As one passes through the concrete wall that surrounds the town, there is much to appreciate within.

The Church of the Nativity, saved
by its mosaic façade . . .

In spite of the fact that the town was a ruin during Bridget's time, the Church of the Nativity had survived and was the same church that Helen ordered to be built in 326. The choir was rebuilt by Emperor Justinian in 540. It was a miracle that the church had not been destroyed by the Persians, who besieged the country in 612 and destroyed all the other churches, including the Church of the Holy Sepulchre. Why did they not destroy the Church of the Nativity? The fact is that they were impressed by its Byzantine mosaic façade that Emperor Justinian had installed when restoring the church. It showed the three Magi in Persian dress!

"They are dressed as we," the conquerors exclaimed, and thus spared the church. It is thought that the wise men were Persian astrologers, wearing their country's national dress.

Today, the mosaic has gone, probably worn away through time, but the church is still there, and it looks more or less as it always has. For that reason, it is certainly true that the basilica with its four rows of 12 columns each, is the best-preserved building from Constantine's and Justinian's time in the Holy Land.

To get an idea about how the mosaic may have looked, we have to go to Ravenna in Italy and visit the Basilica di Sant'Appolinare Nuovo which dates from the first part of the sixteenth century, which also has a mosaic of the Magi in Persian dress! The Ravenna mosaic is from the same period and, like Bethlehem, belonged to the same empire ruled by Emperor Justinian. The mosaics, if not identical, were very much alike.

Muslim devotion in Bethlehem

The church in Bethlehem also survived the massive destruction that the caliph Al-Hakim ordered in 1009. Muslims venerate the place where Jesus was born; they consider him to be one of the greatest prophets, and they also believe in the virgin birth.

Shared between different churches

As a result of the negotiations between the king and queen of Naples and the Egyptian sultan, the whole structure was administered by the Franciscans, the birth grotto from 1333 and the church from 1347. The agreement granted also that oriental denominations could celebrate Mass, each on its own wooden altar. Muslim doorkeepers collected an entrance fee from pilgrims, though today this no longer happens. Pilgrims have to bend very low to enter the church, as the door is only 1.20 metres high. It was built so low during the seventeenth century to prevent anyone from entering the church on horseback. For that reason, it is often called "The Door of Humility".

Today the site is administered equally by Roman Catholics, Greek Orthodox and Armenians.

Inside the Church of the Nativity

During Bridget's visit, it was possible to admire paintings and mosaics created by Crusaders during the middle of the twelfth century. Among the paintings of saints between the columns, Bridget and her company were pleased to see two Scandinavian kings: Knut of Denmark and Olof of Norway. Mural mosaics on a golden background showed Jesus' family tree according to Matthew and Luke, and the seven ecumenical synods were represented. The sanctuary was decorated with mosaics representing scenes from Jesus' life. Today it is still possible to see traces of them.

Jesus' birthplace

The place where Jesus was born is in the cave, once used as a stable, situated below the high altar. One reaches it via a curved staircase. Down in the apse there is a golden star, indicating the exact place where the Virgin Mary gave birth to Jesus. The star has 14 points, symbolizing the 14 generations between King David and Jesus, recognizing Jesus as the

Messiah and the king of Israel. Nearly opposite, a few steps down, there is the part of the grotto where the crib was located.

Queen Helena made a lateral chapel in the cave where she put a silver crib. It was stolen by the Persians during their invasion in 612. According to a traveller's description from the fourteenth century, there was a column walled in inside the lateral chapel, on which Mary was leaning when she gave birth to Jesus. There is also the place where Jesus rested his head and which yielded and became as soft as a pillow when Jesus put his arm there. There used to be a marble slab on which Mary ate food together with the three wise men, but it is not there now.

On the way down to the crypt, today you can still see the mosaic in Byzantine style representing Jesus' birth. Mary is on a bed and Jesus is wrapped in swaddling clothes, while the donkey and the ox are nearby. The shepherds receive the good news, the wise men travel on their journey, guided by the star.

This way of representing Jesus' birth would soon be changed by Bridget according to her personal experience on the spot.

The vision of the birth of Jesus

The promise that Bridget received on her way between Alvastra and Vadstena—that she should come to the Lion, the place where Jesus, also called the Lion of Judah, was born—was now fulfilled. When Bridget was still in Rome, Mary had promised to disclose how the holy birth happened so that Mary remained a virgin even after the birth. When she was in Naples, Bridget had caught a glimpse of what should happen once she was in Bethlehem. Now this moment had finally come.[44]

Bridget sees the whole birth happen. Angels, shepherds, the ox and the donkey are there, Joseph is bringing a candle and Mary takes off her shoes and puts them behind her. Joseph leaves the cave. Mary goes down on her knees. And suddenly, at the very moment of birth, Jesus is there in the middle of the floor, naked and shining like the sun. Everything was so quick. How did Jesus come out? How was it that Bridget could

---

[44] Book 7, Chapter 22.

not see it happen? Jesus' coming was a miracle. And Mary pronounced with reverence the following words: "Be welcome, my God, my Lord, my Son."[45]

Theologians have often debated Bridget's vision of Jesus' birth. It could be compared with a "spiritual Caesarean section", corresponding to the annunciation. That was the reason why Joseph left and that there was no place in the inn. When God transformed himself into a human being, nobody is allowed to be present. That Mary gave birth without pain had been confirmed in a shorter revelation, when Mary told Bridget: "I gave birth to him with such a spiritual happiness and delight that I did not feel any discomfort or pain when he left my body."[46]

This vision, to which we will return when Bridget stays in Naples on her way back to Rome, would revolutionize artistic representations of Jesus' birth, at least in the West, where it would break long-held traditions among artists who portrayed the scene.

Earlier, Jesus was always represented in swaddling clothes with Mary seated holding him in her arms, or lying or sitting close to him. But after Mary's revelation to Bridget became known, artists in the West began to paint Jesus naked on the floor, with Mary standing behind.

The description of Jesus in the manger, portrayed in Luke's Gospel, (Luke 2:1–20) is certainly correct, but what Mary wanted to show Bridget is exactly how everything happened when Jesus was born. One description does not exclude the other. Luke is describing the moment after the delivery, when Jesus was swaddled and placed in the manger, after which Mary can rest. Bridget, on the other hand, describes the moment of delivery.

---

[45]   Book 7, Chapter 21.

[46]   Book 7, Chapter 22.

The visits of the shepherds and the wise men

Through the Virgin Mary, Bridget also learned that if Bethlehem had
not been so crowded for the Roman census and taxation with which
everyone was preoccupied, the news about Jesus' birth would have spread
much further. In a revelation, Bridget saw the shepherds arriving. When
they had heard that a Saviour had been born, they wanted to be sure that
it was a boy in the manger and not a girl, and Mary showed them her son.
They prayed to him immediately with great veneration.[47]

In the following revelation, Mary describes the visit of the wise
men; she was surprised when they entered and worshipped Jesus. Jesus
himself was very happy about this distinguished visit and Mary was also
delighted. Bridget too shared in their happiness.[48]

The Church of St Catherine and the Cave of St Jerome

The Church of the Nativity is connected to several caves which, in turn,
are connected with the Church of St Catherine. As early as the twelfth
century, there was a small church in this location. When the Franciscans
arrived in Bethlehem in 1347, they based themselves there and dedicated
the church to the early Christian saint Catherine of Alexandria. The
church has been rebuilt and enlarged several times, lastly in 1881. One
of the chapels is devoted to St Joseph, at the place where he received
a warning from an angel to escape to Egypt. The Chapel of the Holy
Innocents is devoted to the children from Bethlehem who were killed
by Herod in his effort to be rid of the infant Jesus.

In one of these caves the church father Jerome (ca 347–420) lived
for 35 years. There he translated both the Old and the New Testaments
into Latin, the so-called *Versio Vulgata*. There is a statue of Jerome in the
forecourt of the church, dating back to the time of the Crusaders.

Another noteworthy monument which was shown to Bridget's group
was a well inside a cave. According to legend, the star guiding the three

---

47   Book 7, Chapter 23.
48   Book 7, Chapter 24.

wise men was said to have fallen into the well after the wise men arrived at the manger. The guides told the credulous pilgrims that if they looked very carefully inside the well, they could still see the star at the bottom.

The Milk Grotto

A hundred metres east of the Church of the Nativity, is the so-called Milk Grotto. According to tradition, the holy family had been hiding there for 40 days during King Herod's slaughter of the children of Bethlehem. Legend has it that when the Virgin Mary happened to spill her milk on the rock, it turned white and from then on possessed healing properties. Today pilgrims can buy a packet containing white powdered stone from the grotto, and expectant mothers pray at the rock that they will have plenty of milk for their children. The chapel in the Milk Grotto was built in 1872 on the foundations of a church from the fourth century.

The Shepherds' Field

East and not far from Bethlehem is the field where the shepherds saw and heard the message of the angels on the night that Jesus was born. It is close to the village Beit Sahour. Here and there are remainders left of Byzantine buildings and of caves used by the shepherds. One of the bigger caves is used as a chapel where a crib is left all year round. It is certainly the only place in the world where you can celebrate Christmas every day!

A modern church was built there in 1950 which is well worth a visit. It is meant to remind you of a shepherd's tent and the light coming inside the church through the cupola is meant to be the light shining on the shepherds the night when the angels announced that Messiah was born.

Staying in Bethlehem

It is not known where Bridget and her party stayed overnight in Bethlehem, but they would not have returned to Jerusalem the same day. Even in those days there was accommodation there for pilgrims; it may also be possible that Bridget spent the night praying in the Grotto of the Nativity.

There is no lack of accommodation in Bethlehem today. Besides the 30 hotels in all price ranges, in 2002 the Bridgettine Sisters opened a guest house—Mary's House or Hosh Al-Qattan—with 13 rooms and 28 beds. It is situated only ten minutes' walk from the Church of the Nativity.

1 3

Back home from the Holy Land

Summer was almost over, and Bridget was longing to return home. She had visited the five places mentioned in the *Book of Questions*, and the Virgin Mary's promise to show "how everything happened in Bethlehem" had been fulfilled. She would like to have visited Galilee, Lake Gennesaret and the town of Nazareth where Jesus grew up. But travelling to the northern places of the Holy Land was out of the question, as it was considered very dangerous.

In the meantime, Bridget fell ill with a fever and pains in her stomach. She wanted to return home, but as was her habit she did not want to take any decisions without having first received a direct order or hint about what she should do. So, on 8 September, the birthday of Our Lady, she visited her tomb outside the Lion Gate in Jerusalem and finally received the right order at the right time: she should now return home. "You shall now return to the countries of the Christians; always improve your life and try to live with the greatest care and attention, now that you have visited the holy places where my Son and I have lived physically, died and been buried."[49]

---

[49]   Book 7, Chapter 26.

Back to Cyprus

The journey to Jaffa

The pilgrims probably left Jerusalem on 20 September. Their first stop was Rama, about 40 kilometres west. By starting early in the morning, it was possible to complete the distance in one day. Bridget stayed overnight in one of the lodgings in the town, and there had the opportunity to talk to a man who had apostatized from his Christian faith, probably to convert to Islam. After the conversation with Bridget, he promised that he should return to the faith of his childhood and never again consider false teachings.

Once in Jaffa, the group had to wait until the sea and the wind became more favourable, so that they could leave for Famagusta in Cyprus. They arrived at Cyprus at the beginning of October. The town was more crowded than usual as preparations for the coronation of the young Peter II to become king of Jerusalem were under way, an event that would be attended by many invited guests.

But Bridget had something else on her mind. When she still was in Jerusalem, she had had a revelation with a message for the young king of Cyprus and his uncles. It also included sharp warnings for the city's inhabitants. The message had been sent to them earlier through the Franciscan friar, Martin of Aragon. The king and his family chose to ignore the message and the warning, and for that reason, Bridget decided that, on her arrival, she should make it public as soon as possible. The revelation was read on 8 October, only four days before the coronation. The place chosen was outside the royal castle in Famagusta, which was of great strategic importance.

Many of the citizens came to listen to the message, and Bridget delivered a long and severe lecture to them. The revelation was directed both to the "Latin Christians", i.e. Catholics, and to "the Greeks", i.e. the Greek Orthodox people. The Catholics were accused of following their own will, doing whatever they wanted and not fearing God. The Greeks were accused of not being obedient to the only Church, i.e. the Catholic Church, and to the pope who was Christ's vicar on earth.

The consequence of the disobedience would be the following: the Catholics would be annihilated from the island and within a short time be forgotten. On the other hand, the Orthodox should know that their country would never live in peace and that the enemy should cause them injury and misery.[50]

Riots in Famagusta

The revelation was received with mixed feelings. It was an unpleasant truth that Bridget presented, but in spite of people's reaction to it, trouble for the people of Cyprus began only four days later during the coronation on 12 October. A dispute between the representatives of the sea republics of Genoa and Venice arose, resulting in a fight near to the king during the coronation.

During the banquet that followed, there was another confrontation that ended in a bigger fight, with a number of people injured and dead. The mob attacked and besieged the quarter where the Genoese people lived. Offended, they left the island, but only to return to Genoa and plot their revenge. One of the witnesses of the riot was the royal chamberlain, Peter Malansel from Genoa, who himself was stabbed four times with a dagger. While the doctors pronounced him dead, Bridget, through Bishop Alphonse, sent a message that he should survive, which he did. For that reason, he was later called as a witness in Bridget's canonization.

Now Bridget had done her part. She left the situation in the hands of the people of Cyprus and on 17 October, after having witnessed with grief how her prophecies were beginning to be fulfilled, it was time to leave Cyprus and sail towards Italy. We do not know which route the boat took, but it probably stopped in Rhodes before sailing in the direction of Syracuse on the eastern shore of Sicily.

[50]   Book 7, Chapter 19.

The destiny of Cyprus

After the riots in Cyprus, the Genoese sent immediately seven galleys in order to occupy the strategic places of the island. Later, in 1373, invited by Queen Eleanor, they invaded Cyprus with an armada of 43 galleys and 14,000 soldiers. The queen's intention was to allow Genoa, a powerful trade and shipping power, to occupy Cyprus in order to be able to remove her brothers-in-law John and James, who had been implicated in the murder of her husband, from the administration.

With the help of John of Morf, the titular king of Edessa and also the alleged lover of the queen, Genoa did invade the island, with the result that John was killed on order from Eleanor and James was sent to prison in Genoa in 1374, where he later died.

It took more than a century for the Venetians to have their revenge. In 1489, they took control of the island. But less than a century later, in 1571, during a bloody attack, the island became part of the Ottoman Empire, which banished all Catholics. Nevertheless, the Orthodox were allowed to stay, but they lived with great difficulties. A number of churches, including St Nicholas' Cathedral in Famagusta, were transformed into mosques and are still used as such.

After the British Mandate Period (1878–1960), Cyprus became an independent nation. But there is still unrest; the island was divided in 1974 between Greeks and Turks. It may be that Bridget's revelations have come true in our own time. And Famagusta is an abandoned city: "Therefore, their walls will fall down, the town will be left empty and devastated and its inhabitants will leave it and sigh with grief and sorrow . . ."[51]

---

[51] Book 7, Chapter 70.

Syracuse

The boat sailed to Syracuse on the east coast of Sicily, where it arrived at the end of October. The pilgrims stayed there only three days, but long enough to visit the Norman church of St John and pray in the catacombs, in the same place where, according to local tradition, St Paul 13 centuries earlier had given thanks after a safe voyage.

1 4

Back to Naples and Rome

A miraculous cross

The boat trip to Naples went without problems. When Bridget had landed in Naples, she presented golden crosses that she had bought in the Holy Land to some of her friends. Some of these crosses were mentioned in her canonization. Associated with them there was a letter to Bridget's daughter Katarina from Queen Johanna, in which she tells her about a miracle that occurred after Bridget's death. The son of the marquis of Monferrato had been declared practically dead by the doctors. When the queen touched him with one of the golden crosses that Bridget had given her, and after having invoked Bridget, the boy's health was restored.

A certain knight named Antonio di Carletto also received such a cross. He placed it on the body of his seriously sick friend Andriolo Mormulos, whose health was immediately restored.

Accusing the Neapolitans

Even though Queen Johanna received such a gift, it did not prevent her from allowing a theological commission to examine Bridget's revelations. They had caused considerable irritation, and there were some people who thought that she was overstepping the mark. Bridget had been criticizing the vanity of the Neapolitans: the women made themselves up too much and dressed in expensive clothes.[52] She also did not like the fact that the Neapolitans owned slaves. Her father, in his role as

---

[52]   Book 7, Chapter 27.

regional administrator, had been one of the members who instituted the Uppland law in 1296, which among other things prohibited slavery. Even worse, the Neapolitans did not baptize their slaves or instruct them in the Christian faith as, if they were Christians, they could not be slaves.

In the same revelation the Neapolitans were accused of turning to fortune tellers and witches for advice over many aspects of their lives.[53]

Under house arrest

Bridget's prophecies were examined by a commission composed of Archbishop Bernard, two doctors of canon law and some of the local nobility. They scrutinized Bridget's words and the way in which she had received them, both the prophecies that had been fulfilled and those that were still yet to be. When the commission visited her in her lodging to interrogate her, they found her in a very simple dwelling consisting of one room with a very low bed.

She wanted to return home but had to await the commission's verdict. She was wondering whether the queen should embrace her as her best friend or let her burn at the stake. The commission would decide.

What did Bridget do to pass this long time of waiting? Well, she was doing what she always did. She visited Naples' churches, as she at least was able to move freely. One of these visits would have unsuspected consequences in the world of art.

Meeting Niccolò Di Tommaso

Why did the vision that Bridget received in the Church of the Nativity in Bethlehem spread so quickly in the world of art? While still in Naples it is likely that Bridget visited the church of St Anthony outside the walls and there met the painter Niccolò di Tommaso. Queen Johanna had allowed the church to be built with a hospital annexed to it and had commissioned Niccolò, from Florence, to complete a triptych representing St Anthony

---

surrounded by St Peter, St Francis, John the Evangelist and St Louis of Toulouse. This painting was signed and dated by Niccolò and it can now be seen in the National Museum of San Martino in Naples.

Though he may not be among the best-known artists, Niccolò was a very accomplished painter. There is very little information available about his life, but we know that he was one of the many architects who in 1366 took part in the building of the Cathedral of Florence. There is no doubt that Niccolò was one of the artists who portrayed the new picture of Jesus' birth in Bethlehem.

Bridget may have told Niccolò the story of Jesus' birth as revealed by the Virgin Mary, that Jesus lay on the floor with Mary on her knees in front of him, with Joseph, the angels and the shepherds nearby.

The fact that Niccolò made such a detailed picture of Jesus' birth such a short time after Bridget's return to Naples, and well before Bridget's revelation was published, well after Niccolò's death in 1376, shows that it was likely that he and Bridget met in the church.

There was also a very important deposition made during the canonization process. Bridget's friend, Earl Nicolaus Orsini, testified in 1380 that he had seen a painting showing Jesus' birth as Mary had described it to Bridget. When he was asked where he had seen the painting, he answered: "In the Church of the Antonites in Naples outside the walls."

According to the Bridgettine scholar Birgit Klockars, the statement can be interpreted in two different ways: that the painting had been there before Bridget went to the Holy Land, in which case there must have been other people who had presented Jesus' birth in that way, which could have influenced Bridget. Or, a painter had been inspired by Bridget's vision and painted according to her instructions. According to Klockars, the second interpretation is the most likely. As the painting reproduces not only Bridget's vision but also the visionary herself, the whole question seems to have been settled.

The painting representing Bridget's vision of the nativity

Niccolò di Tommaso created three paintings, all representing Bridget's revelation in the nativity grotto. The first painting is small (44x55 cm), but it is full of significant details. In the grotto, a bare-footed and genuflecting Virgin Mary wears a white dress and has her hair down on her shoulders. Around her head there is a golden halo. Behind her there are her shoes and cloak, at her side the linen bandages to enfold Jesus. The Virgin Mary, while praying, is looking at the naked child on the ground in front of her, who also has a golden halo. On the left side we can see the ox and donkey at the crib, on the right Joseph with his hands crossed on his breast. In the lower right corner kneels Bridget, with a rosary in her hands, as a witness of this great event.

Outside the cave, the dark sky is illuminated by golden stars. The angels in the right corner on the upper side of the painting are dancing, playing, worshipping and informing the shepherds about Jesus' birth. Four seraphs guard the entrance of the cave, keeping guard for God, who is in the middle of the painting, with a crown of star-shaped glory. Speech comes directly from God's mouth, who is saying: "This is my

Son". In the same way, from Mary's mouth are the words: "Be welcome my God, my Lord and my Son." The theological message shows how the virgin birth happened and also who Jesus' real parents are. But perhaps the most interesting part for us is the "eyewitness" Bridget, in a corner of the painting, looking at the wonder of Jesus' birth.

Today, the painting can be seen in the Vatican Museums in Rome.

Bridget's portrait

There is no doubt that this portrait of St Bridget was painted by a person who actually met her and depicted her as she really was. It also gives us a description of how she dressed. She is depicted as a widow wearing a black dress, a white veil and neckerchief. Behind her there are a walking stick with a pilgrim hat hanging on it and a suitcase; we see her as she was dressed and what she used and took with her during her pilgrimage. Her black dress and white veil is a more authentic outfit than those shown in the later pictures which depicted Bridget in a Bridgettine or even Franciscan habit. Furthermore, Bridget's Nordic features, her worn face and thin body stand out in this portrait. Here we have the real Bridget, as she looked when travelling the streets and visiting the churches in Naples, while waiting for the verdict of the judicial commission. It is not a picture of the robust matron that we see in the abbey of Vadstena.

The Revelations for Gregory XI

It took time for the commission to complete their investigation, which would set Bridget free from every suspicion of heresy and calumny. In the meantime, she could work on the project that was nearest to her heart: the pope's permanent return to Rome.

His name was now Gregory XI and Bridget had great expectations that he would come back to Rome, something that he had revealed as his intention at his installation. Everything was ready and even the date of his departure had been established as May 1373, more or less the same time as Bridget's arrival in Jerusalem. But his cardinals managed to dissuade him. To them Rome was a chaotic town, even, they joked, a place where bad wine was served. Also the French king, who wanted for obvious reasons to keep control over the pope, was against the departure. The project was therefore shelved for the moment.

In spite of this, to Bridget it was now the right time to try to convince Gregory XI to return. She was persuaded, of course, through divine revelations: we know of three of these given to her in Naples.

The first, received on 26 January 1373, is a dialogue between Bridget and Christ, during which Bridget, overcome with exhaustion, explains the reasons why so far the pope has been prevented from returning to Rome. But Christ explains to Bridget that the pope is powerless and compares his condition with that of a paralysed man, plagued by blood poisoning and fever. He adds that the pope loves his own self more than anything else and is lacking in feeling in the presence of Christ. But Christ explains that thanks to the Virgin Mary's intercession, Gregory has already started to change; he wants to follow Christ's wish and honour him by returning to Rome.[54]

The second revelation, written down in February, was produced as a letter to the pope. Jesus, in sharp words, urges the pope to put an end to corruption and profanity which damage the Church. He should also as soon as possible return to Rome; he can decide about the time of his departure, but the sooner he returns the more the Holy Spirit's gifts will be given to him. He is told: "So come without delaying anymore."[55]

The third revelation is also presented as a letter. It was written after Bridget returned to Rome and was sent in July just before her death to Bishop Alphonse, who was then in Avignon, asking him to announce the contents of the pope's letter.

As in the earlier revelations, the pope is exhorted to return to Rome, but this time was added, "You may come in autumn." It starts by confirming the pope's uncertainty about the return. He asks for a sign. But Jesus says: even the Pharisees asked for it and got the sign of the prophet Jonah who escaped from the belly of the fish after three days. In the same way, the pope receives these signs:

---

[54]   Book 4, Chapter 141.

[55]   Book 4, Chapter 142.

"The first is that he has to accept my admonition to redeem souls.

The second is that if he does not return to Rome, he will lose not only his worldly but also his spiritual authority.

The third sign is 'the woman through whom God speaks wonderful words'". And who can that woman be but Bridget?

The message is clear and cannot be misinterpreted. "Even if everybody is dissuading the Pope from coming to Rome and hindering him as much as they can, he shall trust only me and I will help him, and nobody else will have power over him."[56]

It is possible that Bridget, when she received this revelation, was thinking of the harbour in Jaffa, which was associated with the prophet Jonah, who was swallowed by a big fish.

Not guilty

The verdict of the commission arrived in March and, as expected, Bridget was judged not guilty. According to the men of the Church, it was God's words she pronounced and nothing else was expected of her. And with this endorsement, the sick and elderly Bridget could return to her home in Rome.

When the queen understood that Bridget was short of money, she wanted to give her some. Bridget was uncertain whether to accept money from a person who had in many ways treated her badly, but Jesus told her she should not repay good with evil! Even if the queen had a cold heart, Bridget should "receive her gift with love and respect and pray for her so that she will know divine love".[57] Bridget accepted the gift.

Just before her departure Bridget received another gift. In the Convent of the Holy Cross, a nun named Chiara had received from Queen Sancha of Mallorca (1285–1345) some hair which had belonged to the Virgin Mary. Some days before her death, Chiara presented it to Bridget.

---

56   Book 4, Chapter 143.

57   *Extravagantes*, Chapter 110.

Katarina the Turk

Just after Bridget left Naples another gift was sent to her, a female slave! The queen had set free a young Muslim woman, who in the *Diarium Vadstenense* was mentioned as "the Turk". She had been abducted from her country and sold as a slave to Queen Johanna. The queen was moved by Bridget's attitude towards slavery together with the fact that the Church commission had considered Bridget to be right in the things she said. But when the young woman arrived in Rome some months later, Bridget had died. The former slave became a nun in Vadstena and received the Swedish name Katarina Magnusdotter. She died there in 1414.

Bridgettine churches in Naples

Bridget has a devoted following in Naples even today, although there are now only two churches dedicated to her since Santa Brigida dei Calafati was demolished in 1893. One is Santa Brigida a San Luigi, dating from the eighteenth century and situated on the panoramic Via Petrarca. The other, better known, church is Santa Brigida in the centre of the town, on the street with the same name. Bridget's image has also been reproduced in Naples on many frescos and paintings created in the seventeenth century. The most interesting is the bust-sized bronze reliquary, representing Bridget with a crown and sceptre. The explanatory notice with an inaccurate text in Italian saying "St. Bridget, Queen of Sweden" has now been replaced with the more truthful "Saint Bridget, Patron of Europe". In front of the bust there are always fresh flowers donated by the Neapolitans, who in this show their veneration to Bridget and keep her memory alive. The Bridgettine Sisters do the same: in 1999, they took over the sixteenth-century Camaldolense convent on the Camaldoli Hill, from where they have a wonderful view of Naples, the Gulf of Naples and Mount Vesuvius.

The way back home

Bridget's road back to Rome again followed the Via Appia. She made a stop in Nola in order to pray at the tomb of St Paul. The earl of the town visited her, asking her to take care of one of his people, the widow Picciolella of Nola, who for a long time had felt herself buffeted by evil. The widow was taken to Bridget, who ordered her to confess all her sins since childhood and the next day to receive Christ's body and blood. The widow did what Bridget said, and as a gift she received a ribbon, which had been placed on the Holy Sepulchre, and three beads from Bridget's rosary. She was released from her spiritual trouble and temptations and thanked God and Bridget for her gifts.

Back to Rome

The pilgrims arrived back in Rome at the Palatium Magnum at Campo de' Fiori at the beginning of April. The round trip from Rome to Jerusalem and back had reached its end. For more than 16 months the pilgrims had been travelling. Now they had all returned except Charles, who had died in Naples. Bridget could return to her old room, Bishop Alphonse could go back to his library, master Peter and prior Peter to their spiritual charges and the maids to their domestic duties. Everything was now back to normal, and everybody felt a deep gratitude for everything they had experienced during the eventful and sometimes dramatic pilgrimage.

Before Bridget returned to her daily chores, she wanted to pay two of her old friends a visit and tell them what she had experienced during the trip. These were Earl Latino Orsini, who had accompanied them for part of their trip south, and Gomez of Albornos, prefect of the Duchy of Spoleto.

Bridget's last Revelation

Back in Rome, Bridget was exhausted and ill, and stayed at home for most of the time in her Palatium Magnum apartment. Some months later she received her last revelation, informing her that she would die five days later, on the morning of 23 July. In that revelation, Bridget's mission as a prophetess was confirmed, a grace that was given her through her revelations, and the means by which the pope would return to Rome.

In the same revelation, Bridget was informed that "You are dressed as a nun in front of my altar and ordained as such. And you shall from now on be considered not only as my bride but also as a nun and mother in Vadstena."

So even though her imminent death would hinder Bridget from physically reaching Vadstena to become the abbess, she became, through the revelation, consecrated to the office and her body would later be buried in Vadstena.

Bishop Alphonse's addition ends the revelation by saying: "On the fifth day, early in the morning, Christ came again to her, comforting her. After mass had been read and she had taken the sacraments in a devotional spirit of veneration, she expired in the arms of the already mentioned people."[58]

Bridget's life, which started with a revelation that prophesied her mission as a pilgrim and prophetess, ended with a revelation that confirmed her role and achievement.

What happened next

A little more than four months later, Bridget's mortal remains were taken across Europe during a funeral procession of nine months. On 4 July 1374, the procession reached Vadstena and Bridget was buried in the chapel that had been built before the larger convent church was completed.

---

[58] Book 7, Chapter 31.

Bridget was finally in the convent in Vadstena that she had started to build, but which she was unable to see while she was still alive. There were other people, like her daughter Catherine, who continued her work. Catherine would later be glad to know that the pope had finally returned to Rome on 17 January 1377, and that a year later he approved the rule of Bridget's order.

There were some people who did not believe in the authenticity of Bridget's revelations, but the commission of enquiry confirmed that their contents corresponded to the doctrine of the Church. On 7 October 1391, Bridget was canonized by Pope Boniface IX during a magnificent ceremony in St Peter's Basilica.

After the Reformation, the convent was closed, but in 1935 the Bridget Sisters were able to establish themselves again in Vadstena, where they have a beautiful guesthouse with a view of Lake Vättern.

Conclusion

Encouraged by "the five promises", Bridget undertook the trip to "the five places" to receive "the five-fold fruits". What were the five fruits? What was the result of the trip? It is important to remember that even if the Holy Land was a destination in itself, it was also part of a larger context: the journey from Rome to Jerusalem and back. Although the stay in the Holy Land lasted about four and a half months, the whole trip took over 11 months. And it was especially during the voyage that Bridget was most active as a prophetess, spiritual guide and mediator.

The greatest consequence of her trip was probably the vision of Jesus' birth, which would change its depiction among Western artists. Every time we see a Christmas crib with a naked Jesus and a Mary on her knees, we know that behind it there is Bridget's vision. It may be more difficult to judge the direct and actual effects of Bridget's mediation when it comes to political or religious conflicts in, for instance, Naples or Cyprus. But we know that her presence as a prophetess, with her deep knowledge of theology and politics, had a positive effect. She worked for unity among the Franciscans, for the unity of the universal Church with the pope as a given leader and for classical Christian unity. She could also confirm Jesus' birth, crucifixion, resurrection and ascension, as well as that of the Virgin Mary, and the apostles' and the martyrs' roles to be part of the unbroken faith tradition of the Church.

Bridget could also demonstrate, through her revelations, that the events of Jesus' life on earth had actually happened in the Holy Land. She came to the timeless "five places, empty of pride and burning with love".

But how can the five-fold fruit be identified? It was made more evident as late as 1999, when Bridget was proclaimed Patron of Europe together with St Catherine of Siena and St Teresa Benedicta of the Cross (Edith Stein). Her standing is based on her love of the Church, her courage in the face of opposition from church dignitaries, her caring for people, her ardent but down-to-earth piety, and her achievements directed towards peace in Europe. These fruits, five in number, were seen especially during Bridget's trip to the Holy Land and would continue through her long life. The prophecy from Bridget's birth, that her voice would be heard all over the world, was fulfilled not only during her life but continues in ours.

Bridget's journey to the Holy Land in her own words

Part 1: The dream of the Holy Land

Extravagantes:66 Mary promises that Bridget will come to the Holy Land
About 1342 on the way home from the pilgrimage of Santiago in Spain, probably in the town of Arras in northern France

Mary speaks: "I am the queen of heaven and the mother of sinners. I want to show you what my Son was like as a human being and what happened when he suffered on the cross. And this will be a sign to you, that you will come to the places where I was myself, and there you will see my Son with your spiritual eyes."

Book 5:13 God the Father describes the symbolism of the holy places in the Holy Land
Sometime between 1344 and 1349 on the way from Alvastra to Vadstena

God the Father speaks: "There was a lord whose servant said to him: 'See, your fallow land has been ploughed and the roots have been pulled out. When will the wheat be sown?' The lord answers him: 'Although the roots look as though they have been pulled out, there still remain some old stubble and stumps that will be loosened in the spring by rain and wind. Therefore wait patiently until sowing time comes!' The servant answers: 'What shall I do then between spring and harvest?' The lord says: 'I know five places. All those who go to them receive fivefold fruit, if they come pure and empty of pride and burning with love. In the first place, there was a vessel closed and not closed, a vessel small and not small, a vessel bright and not bright, a vessel empty and not empty, a vessel clean and not clean. In the second place, a lion was born that was seen and not seen, heard and not heard, touched and not touched, acknowledged and unknown, held and not held. In the third place, there was a lamb that was shorn and not shorn, a lamb wounded and not wounded, a lamb crying and not crying, a lamb suffering and not suffering, a lamb dying and not dying.

'In the fourth place, a snake was placed that lay and did not lay, moved and did not move, heard and did not hear, saw and did not see, sensed and did not sense. In the fifth place, there was an eagle that flew and did not fly, came to a place from which it had never departed, rested and did not rest, was renewed and was not renewed, rejoiced and did not rejoice, was honoured and was not honoured.'"

Explanation and clarification of the above images

The Father speaks: "That vessel about which I told you was Mary, daughter of Joachim, mother of Christ's humanity. She was a vessel closed and not closed: closed to the devil but not to God. Just as a stream that is unable to enter a vessel that stands in its way seeks other entries and outlets, so the devil, with all his stratagems, wanted to get near the heart of Mary. But he was never able to incline her spirit to the least little sin, for she was closed to his temptation, since the stream of my Spirit had flowed into her heart and filled her with a special grace.

"Second, Mary, the mother of my Son, was a vessel small and not small: small and modest in the humility of her lowliness, but great and not small in my divine love. Third, Mary was a vessel empty and not empty: empty of every lust and sin, not empty but full of heavenly sweetness and every goodness. Fourth, Mary was a vessel bright and not bright: bright, since every soul is created beautiful by me, but the soul of Mary grew to such a perfection of light that my Son dwelt in her soul, in the beauty of which heaven and earth rejoiced. But this vessel was not bright among men, in that she scorned the honours and riches of the world.

"Fifth, Mary was a vessel clean and not clean: truly clean because she is all beautiful, and there was not so much uncleanness in her as to fit on the point of a needle. But the vessel was not clean in the sense that she came from the race of Adam and was born of sinners, though she herself was conceived without sin in order that my Son might be born of her without sin. So whoever comes to that place where Mary was born and raised will not only be cleansed but will become a vessel for my honour.

"The second place is Bethlehem, where my Son was born like a lion. His human nature was seen and held but his divine nature was not seen and held.

"The third place is Calvary where my Son was crucified and died like an innocent lamb according to his human nature, but remained immortal according to his divine nature.

"The fourth place was the garden in which was my Son's tomb, and where his human nature was buried, but his divine nature did not confine him there.

"The fifth place was the Mount of Olives from which my Son ascended in his human nature like an eagle to heaven where he ever is, according to his divine nature. He was raised and renewed in his human nature, although he had always been the same according to his divine nature.

"Therefore, whoever comes clean and with a good and perfect intention to these places will see and taste the sweetness and goodness of me, God. And when you come to these places, I will show you more."

Book 7:1 The Virgin Mary promises Bridget that she will get to experience the miracle of birth in Bethlehem
In Rome sometime in the early 1350s

When Lady Bridget, the bride of Christ, was in Rome and was once absorbed in prayer, she began to think about the Virgin Birth and about the very great goodness of God who had chosen such a pure mother for his Son. And her heart then became so greatly inflamed with love for the Virgin that she said within herself: "O my Lady, Queen of Heaven, my heart so rejoices over the fact that the most high God chose you as his mother and deigned to confer upon you so great a dignity that I would rather choose for myself eternal excruciation in hell than that you should lack one smallest point of this surpassing glory or of your heavenly dignity."

And so, full of the sweetness of love, she was suspended in an ecstasy of mental contemplation. Then the Virgin appeared to her and said, "Be attentive, O daughter: I am the Queen of Heaven. Because you love me with a love so immense, I therefore announce to you that you will go on a pilgrimage to the holy city of Jerusalem at the time when it pleases my Son. From there you will go to Bethlehem; and there I shall show you, at the very spot, the manner in which I gave birth to that same Son, Jesus Christ; for so it has pleased him."

Book 6:108 St Stephen promises Bridget that she should come to Jerusalem
In the Church of St Lawrence Outside the Walls in Rome some years after 1350

Bridget prayed at the tomb of St Stephen outside the walls in Rome and said: "Blessed be you, St Stephen! You have earned the same merit as St Lawrence, for just as he preached to the Gentiles, you preached to the Jews, and just as Lawrence gladly endured the fire, so you gladly endured the stoning. Therefore, you are rightly praised as the foremost among the martyrs."

Then St Stephen appeared and said to her, "I loved God from my youth, for I had parents who cared for the salvation of my soul. But when my Lord Jesus Christ appeared and began to preach, I listened to him with all my heart. Immediately after his ascension, I united with the apostles and served faithfully and humbly in the office entrusted to me. When the Jews blasphemed my Lord Jesus, I was glad to have had an opportunity to speak with them and I rebuked them for their hardness of heart, to the extent that I was prepared to imitate my Lord and die for the truth. But three things worked together for me: the first was my faith. The second was the prayer of the apostles. The third was the suffering and love of my God. Therefore, I now have a threefold blessing. The first is that I constantly see the face and glory of God. The second is that I can do nothing but what the Lord wants. The third is that my joy is endless. And as you rejoice in my glory, my prayer will help you gain greater knowledge of God; the Spirit of God will remain with you, and you will travel to Jerusalem, to the place where I suffered."

Book 7:6   Jesus gives Bridget permission to leave for the Holy Land
In Rome, 25 May 1371, the feast day of St Urban, Pope and Martyr

When Lady Bridget was living in Rome, she was one day at prayer and her mind was lifted up. Christ then appeared to her and spoke to her, saying: "Prepare yourself now to make a pilgrimage to Jerusalem to visit my sepulchre and the other holy places that are to be found there. You will leave Rome when I tell you."

Book 7:9 Jesus assures Bridget the trip is possible for her
In Rome, sometime between 25 May and 23 November 1371

The Son of God speaks to Bridget and says: "Go now and depart from Rome for Jerusalem. Why do you plead your age? I am the Creator of nature; I can weaken or strengthen nature as it pleases me. I will be with you. I will direct your way. I will guide you and lead you back to Rome; and I will provide everything necessary for you, better than you have ever had before."

Book 7:7   The Virgin Mary gives a theological directive to a Franciscan friar
Santa Maria Rotonda (Pantheon) in Rome, 25 November 1371, shortly before leaving for the Holy Land

Honour and thanks be given to almighty God and to the Blessed Virgin Mary, his most worthy Mother! It seemed to me, unworthy person that I am, that while I was absorbed in prayer, the Mother of God spoke to me, a sinner, these following words: "Say to my friend the friar, who through you sent his supplication to me, that it is the true faith and the perfect truth that if a person, at the devil's instigation, had committed every sin against God and then, with true contrition and for the purpose of amendment, truly repented these sins and humbly, with burning love, asked God for mercy, there is no doubt that the kind and merciful God himself would immediately be as ready to receive that person back into his grace with great joy and happiness as would be a loving father who saw returning to him his only, dearly beloved son, now freed from a great scandal and a most shameful death.

"Yes, much more willingly than any human father, the loving God himself forgives his servants all their sins if they repent and humbly ask him for mercy, if they resolve to sin no more, and, with all the longing of their hearts, desire God's friendship above all things.

"Therefore say to that same friar, on my behalf, that because of his good will and my prayer, God in his goodness has already forgiven him all the sins that he ever committed in all the days of his life. Tell him also that, because of my prayer, the love that he has for God will always increase in him until his death and will in no way diminish.

"Likewise, say to him that it pleases God my Son that he should stay in Rome, preaching, giving good advice to those who ask, hearing confessions, and imposing penances, unless his superior should send him sometimes out of the city for some necessary purpose. For their transgressions, the same friar should charitably reprove his other brothers with gracious words, with relevant teaching and, when he is able to correct them, even with just rebukes, so that they may keep the rule and humbly amend their lives.

"Furthermore, I now make known to him that his Masses and his reading and his prayers are acceptable and pleasing to God. And therefore tell him that, just as he guards himself against any excess in food and drink and sleep, so he must diligently guard himself against too much abstinence, in order that he may not suffer any faintness in performing divine duties and services. Also, he is not to have an overabundance of clothing but only necessary things, according to the Rule of Saint Francis, so that pride and greed may not result; for the less costly and valuable his clothes have been, the greater shall be his reward. And let him humbly obey all of his superior's instructions that are not contrary to God and that the friar's own ability permits him to perform.

"Tell him also, on my behalf, what he will answer to those who say that the pope is not the true pope and that it is not the true Body of Jesus Christ my Son that the priests dedicate on the altar. He should answer such heretics in this way: 'You have turned your backs on God, and thus you do not see him. Therefore turn your faces to him, and then you will be able to see him.'

"For a pope who is truly dedicated is part of the true and Catholic faith. No matter how stained he is with other sins and bad deeds, he is never so wicked that there would not always be in him full authority and complete power to bind and loose souls. He possesses this authority through blessed Peter and has acquired it from God. For before Pope John, there were many supreme pontiffs who are now in hell. Nevertheless, the just and reasonable judgements that they made in the world are approved in God's sight.

"For a similar reason, I also say that all those priests who are not heretical—although otherwise full of many other sins—are true priests who handle the Body of Christ my Son at the altar, and they administer the other sacraments even though, because of their sins, they are unworthy of heavenly glory in God's sight."

Book 7:8   The Virgin Mary adds more theological directive to a Franciscan friar

Santa Maria Rotonda (Pantheon) in Rome, 25 November 1371, shortly before leaving for the Holy Land

"Say to my friend the friar that it is not for you to know whether the soul of Pope John XXII is in hell or in heaven. Nor indeed is it for you to know anything about the sins that the same pope took with him when, after his death, he came before God's judgement. But tell the same friar that those decrees that the same Pope John made or established concerning Christ's private property contain no error regarding the Catholic faith, nor any heresy.

"I, indeed, who gave birth to the true God himself, bear witness to the fact that the same Jesus Christ, my Son, had one personal possession. This was that tunic that I made with my own hands. And the prophet witnesses to this fact, saying in the person of my Son: 'Over my garment, they cast lots.' Behold and be attentive to the fact that he did not say 'our garment' but 'my garment'.

"Know too that, as often as I dressed him in that tunic for the use of his most holy body, my eyes then filled at once with tears and my whole heart was wrung with trouble and grief and was afflicted with intense bitterness. For I knew how that tunic would, in the future, be taken from my Son, at the time of his passion when, naked and innocent, he would be crucified by the Jews. And this tunic was that garment over which his crucifiers cast lots. No one had that same tunic while he lived, but only he alone.

"Know too that all those who say that the pope is not the true pope and that the priests are not true priests or rightly ordained and that what is consecrated by the priests in the celebration of Masses is not the true Body of my blessed Son, yes, all those who assert such speak with the spirit of the devil in hell.

"For truly these same heretics have committed such serious sins against God that they are filled with diabolic wickedness, and, through their heresy, they are cut off and cast out from the whole flock of Christianity in the just judgement of God's divine majesty, just as Judas was shut out and cut off from the apostles because of his wickedness: for he betrayed Christ my Son. Know that, even so, all those who seek to amend their lives will obtain mercy from God."

Part 2: On the way to the Holy Land

Book 7:11   Christ invites Queen Johanna to rule justly and to surround herself with good advisers
Naples, sometime between December 1371 and March 1372

"I am God, the Creator of all. I gave free will to angels and to humans so that those who wanted to do my will might remain with me forever, and so that those who were against me might be separated from me. And so, certain of the angels became demons because they did not want to love me or to obey me. Then when man had been created and the devil saw my love for man, the devil not only became my enemy but also promoted war against me by inciting Adam to break my commandments. The devil prevailed on that occasion by my permission and as a result of my justice; and ever since that time, the devil and I are in discord and strife because I want man to live according to my will, while the devil exerts himself to make man follow his own desires.

"Therefore at that moment when I opened heaven with my heart's blood, the devil was deprived of that justice which he seemed to have; and those souls that were worthy were saved and freed. Then the law was established that it should be man's decision to follow me, his God, in order to obtain an everlasting crown. But if he allows himself to succumb to the devil, he will receive everlasting punishment. Thus the devil and I are locked in an endless struggle, since we both desire souls as bridegrooms desire their brides. For I desire souls in order to give them eternal joy and honour; but the devil desires to give them eternal horror and sorrow. Hear what the queen had done to me. I allowed the raising of her to a kingship, etc.

ADDITION

Christ speaks: "Write to her that she should make a complete confession of all that she has done from her youth and that she should be determined to amend her life according to the advice of her confessor. Second, she should diligently recall the manner and the quality of her life during her marriage and her reign; for she will have to render an account of everything to me. Third, she must pay her debts and restore that which she knows was wrongly acquired. For the soul is in peril as long as such things are kept; and it does no good to give lavish gifts if debts go unpaid. Fourth, she is not to burden the community with her new inventions, but instead should lighten people's daily burdens. For God will hear the sighs and the crying of those in misery.

"Fifth, she must have councillors who are just and not covetous; and she must entrust her judgements to such men as love truth and do not fawn upon society's factions or seek to grow rich but know how to be content with only what is necessary. Sixth, every day, at fixed times, she should remember Jesus' wounds and his passion, for by this means the love of God is renewed in the heart. Seventh, at fixed times she should collect the poor, wash their feet, and care for them. She should love all her subjects with sincere charity, bringing all those at strife back together and consoling those who are unjustly treated. Eighth, she should give her gifts with discretion and according to her means, not oppressing some while making others rich, but wisely relieving some without burdening anyone.

"Ninth, she is not to take bribes from rich people, but she should instead pursue justice; setting aside all greed, she is to carefully consider people's crimes and show more compassion where she sees greater humility. Tenth, during her lifetime, she is to apply all her diligence to ensure that she can leave her kingdom in a stable condition when she dies, for I predict to her that henceforth she will not have any children to succeed her. Eleventh, she should be content with the physical attributes which God has given her, for extraneous adornment is very displeasing to God. Twelfth, she is to acquire greater humility and contrition for her sins because, in my eyes, she is careless in her treatment of others, a prodigal squanderer of my gifts, and the cause of tribulation to my friends. Thirteenth, she must have continual fear in her heart, because all her adult life she has behaved like a lascivious woman rather than a queen.

"Fourteenth, she should put aside worldly customs and dismiss those women who flatter her. She should spend the short time that she has left in honouring me, for until now she has treated me as if I were just another human being without recollection of her sins. Let her now fear and live in such a way that she may not feel my judgement. Otherwise, if she does not listen to me, I will judge her not as a queen but as an ungrateful apostate; and I will scourge her from head to heel; and she will be a disgrace before me and my angels and my saints."

Book 7:11   Christ gives advice to the queen how she should deal with two officers in her service
Naples, sometime between December 1371 and March 1372

Christ speaks: "Write these things with fewer and gentler words, just as the Holy Spirit will inspire you, and send them through my bishop to the queen."

Item, concerning a certain queen. A lady was seen standing in a shift spattered with sperm and mud. And a voice was heard: "This woman is like a monkey that sniffs at its own stinking posterior. She has poison in her heart that is harmful to her and she walks into traps that cause her to fall." She was seen wearing a crown of twigs spattered with human excrement and with mud from the streets, and sitting naked on a rotten beam. At once there appeared a most beautiful virgin who said: "This is that insolent and audacious woman who is reputed by mankind to be a woman of the world, but in God's eyes, she has been cast off, as you see." And the virgin added: "O woman, think of your beginning and be attentive to your end; open the eyes of your heart and see that your councillors are those who hate your soul!"

Item, concerning a certain queen. A woman was seen sitting on a golden seat; and two Ethiopians stood before her—one, as it were, on the right and the other on the left. The one standing on the right called out and said: "O lionlike woman, I bring blood. Take and pour out! For it is a mark of the lioness to thirst after blood." The one on the left said: "O woman, I bring to you fire in a vessel. Take—for you are of a fiery nature—and pour out into the waters in order that your memory may last in the waters as well as on the land."

Then a virgin of wondrous beauty appeared, and the Ethiopians fled from her sight. She said: "This woman is in a perilous state. If she prospers in accordance with her own will, the result will be tribulation for many. But if she suffers tribulation, the result will be more useful to her in obtaining eternal life. She herself does not wish to give up her own will, or to suffer tribulation in compliance with God's will. Therefore, if she is left to her own devices, she will not bring consolation to herself or to others."

Item, a revelation. The Son appeared and said: "This woman has done some things that pleased me. Therefore, because of the prayers of my friends, I am willing to point out to her how she may escape people's scorn and the squandering of her own soul if, indeed, she obeys well; if not, she would not escape the justice of the Judge; for she did not will to hear the Father's voice."

Concerning Lord Gomez [Gomes Garcias de Albornoz, diplomat and commander, died in 1377], the Mother of God speaks: "Advise him to do justice wherever he can. If he knows that he has goods that were wrongly acquired, he must not delay in making restitution. He must also be careful not to impose heavy burdens on his subjects, and he must be content with the things that he has because they are sufficient for him if he manages them well and with moderation. Women other than his own wife he must avoid like poison; and he must not lead out the army against anyone nor take part in the action himself unless he knows without doubt that justice is on his side and that the war is just. He must also be zealous in making frequent use of confession and in receiving the Body of Christ more frequently, and in occupying himself, at fixed times of the day, with the remembrance of Christ's passion and his wounds."

Concerning Anthony of Carleto, a merchant in Naples, later in Queen Johanna's service, Christ speaks: "Tell the queen to let him stay in his position. If he rises up to greater things, it will be at the cost of his soul; and neither he himself nor his friends will have any joy from his promotion." And so it all came to pass.

Book 7:12   In Naples Bridget invites Archbishop Bernhard to be moderate and restrained in leading his diocese
Naples, sometime between December 1371 and March 1372

Christ speaks to Bridget and says: "Tell him that if he wishes to be called a bishop in the justice of the divine judgement, he must not imitate the manners and customs of many who are now rulers of the Church. I took on a human body and was born of a virgin in order that by words and deeds I might fulfil the law which, from eternity, had been ordained in the Godhead. I opened the gate of heaven with my heart's blood, and I so illumined the way by my words and deeds that all might use my example in order to merit eternal life. But truly, the words that I said and the deeds that I did in the world are now almost completely forgotten and neglected. For this, no one is as much to blame as the prelates of the churches. They are full of pride, greed, and the rottenness of bodily pleasure.

"All of these things are contrary to my commandments and to Holy Church's statutes, which my friends established from their great devotion after my ascension, when I had accomplished my task in the world. But those wicked prelates of the churches, who are filled with evil spirits, have given people poor examples that are exceedingly harmful; and therefore it is necessary for me to exact full justice from them, abolishing them from the book of life in heaven and placing them beside my enemy Lucifer in hell, which shall be the place of their perpetual torment. Nevertheless, you ought to know that if anyone is willing to amend himself before death by loving me with all his heart, and if he abstains from sins, then I will promptly show my mercy.

"Tell him also, as if these words are your own: "My Lord, it sometimes happens that, from a black furnace, there appears a beautiful flame that is useful and necessary to fashion works of beauty. But that does not mean that the furnace must be praised for its black colour. The praise and honour and thanks are owed to the artist and master of those works.

"It is a similar situation with me, unworthy woman that I am, if you find something useful in my advice; for then you ought continually to show infinite thanks and willing service, not to me, but to God himself, who made and makes all things and who has a perfect will to do good. My Lord, I begin by first speaking to you of those things that relate to the salvation of many souls. I advise you that, if you would have God's friendship, neither you, nor any other bishop acting on your behalf, should be willing to ordain anyone unless he has first been diligently examined by good clerics and has been found to be the right person both in his life and character, so that, by the testimony of wise and truthful men, he is declared worthy to receive such an office.

"With diligent attention, see to it that all the bishops under you and all the suffragans of your archbishopric do the same. For no one would believe how great God's indignation is against those bishops who do not take care to know and diligently to examine the quality of those whom they promote to orders of such dignity in their bishoprics. Whether they do this at the supplication of others or out of negligence and laziness or because of fear, they shall indeed render a most strict account of this at God's judgement.

"I also advise you to inquire about the number and the identities of those holders of benefices in your diocese who have the care of souls. Summon them to your presence at least once a year to discuss with them their own welfare and that of the souls they care for. And if, by chance, they could not all come together on the same day, then definite dates are to be set on which they may come to you individually during the year, so that none of them may be able to excuse himself in any way from consulting you for a whole year.

"And you are to preach to them about the kind of life to be led by those who have an office of such great importance. Know too that priests who have concubines and celebrate Mass are as acceptable and pleasing to God as were the inhabitants of Sodom whom God despatched to hell.

"And even though the Mass, in itself, always is the same and has the same power and efficacy, nevertheless, the kiss of peace that such fornicating priests give in the Mass is as pleasing to God as the kiss by which Judas betrayed the Saviour of all. Therefore constantly try as much as possible, with words and deeds, by enticing, rebuking or threatening, to work together with them so that they may endeavour to lead a chaste life, especially since they must touch such a holy Sacrament and, with their hands, administer it to other faithful Christians.

"Furthermore, for their salvation you should advise all the clergy, both the higher ranks of prelates or canons and also the minor clerics—all, that is, who are subject to your rule and have ecclesiastical incomes—that they should correct their lives in every respect. And let no one believe that, for the sake of avoiding sodomy, fornication is at all permissible for clerics; nor, for that reason, should they defile themselves with women. For every Christian who has the use of intellect and who does not care about eternal life while he is living, will undoubtedly endure after death the most severe punishments of hell for eternity.

"I also advise you that your household should not be over large, but it should be proportionate to the needs of your office as a ruler and to the requirements of your status. Those clerics, therefore, who are called your companions, you should keep with you wherever you may be, for the good of your reputation rather than for vainglory or for pomp; but they are to be few in number rather than many. But those clerics whom you maintain to sing the divine office or to pursue studies or to teach others or to write, you may have as many as you please. And it is to your advantage to take diligent care, as best you can, for their correction and for the salvation of their souls.

"Be attentive to the rest of your servants so that each has his own task; and if some of them are superfluous, do not keep them out of vainglory lest your heart become proud at having a larger household than your peers. It is also expedient that you always consider those truly necessary members of your household whom you keep with you; painstakingly scrutinize their lives like a true householder, correcting their actions, lives, and characters and encourage and admonish them in a fatherly way so that they learn to eschew sins and vices and to love God above all things. It is indeed more acceptable to God and more useful to yourself that you keep with you no member of the household who is unwilling to comply with sound advice and humbly amend his transgressions.

"Regarding your clothing, I advise you never to have in your possession more than three pairs at one time; everything beyond this, you should immediately give to God himself. Of bed covers, towels and tablecloths, keep for yourself only what is necessary and useful to you; and give the rest to God. Of silver vessels, reserve for yourself just enough for your own person and for the guests who eat at your own table; donate the superfluous pieces to God with a cheerful mind. For the rest of your household and the guests who sit at other tables certainly can, without any embarrassment, eat and drink using vessels of tin, clay, wood or glass. For that custom which now prevails in the houses of bishops and lords of having an overly excessive abundance of gold and silver is harmful to souls and repulsive to God himself, who, for our sake, subjected himself to great poverty.

"Beware, also, of having too many courses and extravagant delicacies at meals. Nor should you have overly large and expensive horses, but rather those that are moderate in size and price. Large horses are needed by those who face the dangers of war for the defence of justice and the protection of life, and not for pride. Indeed, I tell you that as often as prelates, out of pride and vainglory, mount big horses, the devil mounts the prelates' necks. For I know a person who, when the prelates and cardinals proudly mounted the backs of their big horses, saw demons as Ethiopians who then mounted the necks of the prelates and sat there, laughing. As often as the prelates pompously spurred their horses, the Ethiopians lifted their heads in glee and kicked their heels into the breasts of those horsemen.

"Again, I advise you to have your vicars promise under oath that, while carrying out your business, they will not presume to do anything contrary to justice. And if they later do the opposite, you are to rebuke in accordance with justice. If you do as I have said, you can be confident that your conscience is clear.

"And now I give advice for the consolation of the souls of your departed, about whom you asked me whether or not they were in purgatory and what alms deeds ought to be done for them, etc. I answer and say that every day for one year you are to celebrate two Masses for them and every day you are to feed two paupers, and every week take care to distribute one florin in coins to the poor.

"Say also to the parish priests that they are to correct their parishioners and to rebuke them for their sins in cases that pertain to them, in order that they may be able to live better lives. Those parishioners who are unwilling to be rebuked should then be rebuked by you. If, however, you know that some are openly sinning against God and his justice, and if they are so stubborn that you cannot pass judgement on them, then tell them in sweet and gentle words to amend themselves.

"If they do not wish to obey, you may leave them to God's judgement; and God will see that your intention is good. One must not throw the meek lamb into a wolf's ferocious teeth because this will make the wolf more ravenous. Nevertheless, it is fitting for you to forewarn them charitably about the peril of their souls, as a father does his children when they oppose him. Nor are you bound to forego rebukes out of fear for your safety unless, by chance, they could be a danger to others."

Book 7:10   In Naples Bridget warns Archbishop Bernhard from allowing marriage for priests
Naples, sometime between December 1371 and March 1372

Rejoice eternally, O blessed Body of God, in perpetual honour and in perennial victory and in your everlasting omnipotence together with your Father and the Holy Spirit and also with your blessed and most worthy Mother and with all your glorious heavenly court. To you be praise indeed, O eternal God, and endless thanksgiving for the fact that you deigned to become a human being, and that for us in the world you willed to consecrate your venerable Body out of material bread, and lovingly bestowed it on us as food for the salvation of our souls!

It happened that a person who was absorbed in prayer heard then a voice saying to her: "O you to whom it has been given to hear and see spiritually, hear now the things that I want to reveal to you: namely, concerning that archbishop who said that if he were pope, he would give leave for all clerics and priests to contract marriages in the flesh. He thought and believed that this would be more acceptable to God than that clerics should live dissolutely, as they now do. For he believed that through such marriage the greater carnal sins might be avoided; and even though he did not rightly understand God's will in this matter, nonetheless that same archbishop was still a friend of God.

But now I shall tell you God's will in this matter; for I gave birth to God himself. You will make these things known to my bishop and say to him that circumcision was given to Abraham long before the law was given to Moses and that, in that time of Abraham, all human beings were guided according to their own intellect and according to the choice of their own will and that, nevertheless, many of them were then friends of God. But after the law was given to Moses, it then pleased God more that human beings should live under the law and according to the law rather than follow their own human understanding and choice. It was the same with my Son's blessed Body.

For after he instituted in the world this new sacrament of the Eucharist and ascended into heaven, the ancient law was then still kept: namely, that Christian priests lived in carnal matrimony. Nevertheless, many of them were still friends of God because they believed with simple faith that this was pleasing to God: namely, that Christian priests should have wives and live in wedlock just as, in the ancient times of the Jews, this had pleased him in the case of Jewish priests. And so, this was the observance of Christian priests for many years.

"But that observance and ancient custom seemed abominable and hateful to all the heavenly court and to me, who gave birth to his body: namely, because it was being thus observed by Christian priests who, with their hands, touch and handle this new and immaculate Sacrament of the most holy Body of my Son. For the Jews had, in the ancient law of the Old Testament, a shadow, i.e., a figure, of this Sacrament; but Christians now have the truth itself—namely, him who is true God and man—in that blessed and consecrated bread.

"After those earlier Christian priests had observed these practices for a time, God himself, through the inspiration of his Holy Spirit, put into the heart of the pope then guiding the Church another law more acceptable and pleasing to him in this matter, so that he established a statute in the universal Church that Christian priests, who have so holy and so worthy a calling, namely, of consecrating this precious Sacrament, should by no means live in the easily contaminated, carnal delight of marriage.

"And therefore, through God's preordinance and his judgement, it has been justly ordained that priests who do not live in chastity and continence of the flesh are cursed and excommunicated before God and deserve to be deprived of their priestly office. But still, if they truthfully amend their lives with the true purpose of not sinning further, they will obtain mercy from God.

"Know this too: that if some pope concedes to priests a license to contract carnal marriage, God will condemn him to a sentence as great, in a spiritual way, as that which the law justly inflicts in a corporeal way on a man who has transgressed so gravely that he must have his eyes gouged out, his tongue and lips, nose and ears cut off, his hands and feet amputated, all his body's blood spilled out to grow completely cold, and finally, his whole bloodless corpse cast out to be devoured by dogs and other wild beasts. Similar things would happen in a spiritual way to that pope who was to go against the aforementioned preordinance and will of God and concede to priests such a license to contract marriage.

"For that same pope would be totally deprived by God of his spiritual sight and hearing, and of his spiritual words and deeds. All his spiritual wisdom would grow completely cold; and finally, after his death, his soul would be cast out to be tortured eternally in hell, so that there it might become the food of demons everlastingly and without end. Yes, even if St Gregory the Pope had made this statute, in the aforesaid sentence he would never have obtained mercy from God if he had not humbly revoked his statute before his death."

Book 4:44   Christ describes to Bridget how the body can be likened to a ship and the world to a sea

The Son speaks: "Listen, you who long for the harbour after the storms of this world. Whoever is at sea has nothing to fear so long as that person stays there with him who can stop the winds from blowing, who can order any bodily harm to go away and the rocky crags to soften, who can command the storm-winds to lead the ship to a restful harbour. So it is in the physical world.

"There are those who lead the body like a ship across the waters of the world, bringing some people consolation but others distress, for human free will leads some souls to heaven, others to the depths of hell.

"The human will is pleasing to God when it desires to hear nothing more fervently than God's praise nor to live for anything other than God's service, for God dwells happily in such a will and lightens every danger and smoothes away all the rocks by which the soul is often endangered.

"What do these rocks represent if not evil desire? It is delightful to see and own worldly possessions, to rejoice in the elegance of ones' body and to taste whatever delights the flesh. Such things often endanger the soul.

"But when God is on board the ship, all these things grow weak, and the soul scorns them all, for all bodily and earthly beauty is like a glass that is painted on the outside but full of earth on the inside. When the glass gets broken, it is no more useful than the dark soil of the earth, which has been created for no other purpose than to be used, if one owns any, in order to gain heaven.

"All those people who no more desire to know of their own or the world's esteem than they do the noxious air, those who mortify every limb of their body and hate the abominable lust of their flesh, all these can rest here in quiet and wake up with joy, because God is with them at all times."

Book 6:67   The ship's three sections are compared with the world's three ages

The Son speaks: "This world is like a ship full of worries, tossed by the storms of temptation and leaving no man any security or tranquillity until it has reached the port of rest. As the ship has three sections, namely the prow, the middle and the stern, so the world goes through three ages, which I now describe to you. The first was from Adam's time until my birth. This age is denoted by the prow, because it was tall, wonderful and strong. It stood tall through the piety of the patriarchs, wonderful through the wisdom of the prophets, strong in living by the law. But this part gradually began to decline as the Jewish people rejected my commandments and became stained with crime and wickedness. Therefore, they have lost their virtue and property. The middle part of the ship, and the middle part of the world, became visible, when I, the Son of the living God, became human, for as the middle part of the ship is lower and more humble than the other parts, I preached the way of humility and honour and many people understood and lived by it for a long time. But wickedness and pride have now prevailed and my suffering is almost forgotten and lost from memory. The stern, the third part of the ship, is now becoming evident, and it will end in judgement. In this age, I sent the word of my mouth to you through the world, and those who hear and follow it will be blessed. For just as John says in (not in his but my) Gospel: "Blessed are they who have not seen but believed", so I say now: "Blessed are they who hear these words and follow them; yes, eternal bliss they shall win." By the end of this age, the Antichrist will be born. For as by a spiritual marriage the sons of God are born, so the Antichrist is born of a cursed woman, who pretends to understand spiritual things, and of a cursed man; of their seed the devil will, with my permission, do his work. But this Antichrist's time should not be as his brother described it, whose books you have seen, but coincide with a time known to me, when evil exceeded its measure and wickedness grew to great extent. Therefore, you should know that before the Antichrist comes, the door of faith will be opened to pagan people. When Christians then turn their love to heresy, and evil oppresses the priesthood and justice, it is a clear sign that the Antichrist will soon come."

Book 4:88   Well-equipped or inadequate ships compared with the pious and secular human mind

The Son speaks: "I am the creator of all spirits, good and bad. I am also their ruler and helmsman. Moreover, I am the creator of all animals and of each thing that exists and has life, as well as of each thing that exists but does not have life.

Thus, whatever there is in heaven, on earth, or in the sea, each and every one of them is according to my will, except for humankind alone. Know, therefore, that some men are like a boat that has lost both rudder and mast and gets tossed here and there on the swell of the sea until it runs into the cliffs of the island of death. There are on this boat those who, in despair, give their minds over to sensual pleasure.

"Others are like a boat that still has its mast and rudder and an anchor with two cables. However, the main anchor is broken, and the rudder is on the verge of shattering whenever the force of the waves forces itself between the boat and the rudder. Care must therefore be taken because, while the rudder and boat are still connected, they have, as it were, mutual warmth among themselves thanks to that connection.

"The third boat has all its rigging and equipment and is set to sail whenever the right time comes. The first anchor, the main anchor that I mentioned earlier, is religious discipline that is lowered and lightened by the patience and fervour of divine love. This anchor has been shattered, inasmuch as what the Church fathers taught has now been cast underfoot, and instead everyone uses whatever they find useful themselves as a part of the religious profession. They are thus carried about like a boat drifting upon the waves.

"The second anchor, which, as I said, is still in one piece, is the intention of serving God. This is tied by two cables, namely faith and hope, when people believe me to be God and place their hope in my will to save them. I am their rudder, and so long as I am in the boat, the swell of the waves does not enter it, and there exists a warmth between them and me.

"I remain connected to their boat when they love nothing as much as me. I am attached to them by the three nails of godly fear, humility, and the contemplation of my works. But if they love anything more than me, then the water of disintegration enters, the three nails of fear, humility, and divine contemplation disintegrate, the anchor of good will is shattered, and the cables of faith and hope are broken. The people in this boat are in a state of great insecurity and are thus headed for dangerous places.

"My friends are on the third boat because, as I said, it is set for sailing."

Book 7:16   Christ admonishes the people of Cyprus
Famagusta, early May 1372

After this, in that same hour, Christ spoke to Bridget, saying: "To these things that you have now seen and to the other things that I endured, the world's rulers are not attentive; nor do they consider the places in which I was born and where I suffered. For they are like a man who keeps wild and untamed beasts and who sets loose his hunting dogs and takes delight in the pleasure of the chase.

"It is a similar case with the rulers of the earth and the prelates of the churches and all countries of the world. They take great pleasure in earthly delights instead of considering my passion and my death. Therefore, I shall now send them my words through you and, if they do not change and turn their hearts toward me, they will be condemned along with those who divided my clothing and cast lots over my garments."

ADDITION

Here follows a revelation made to blessed Bridget in Famagusta. The Son speaks: "This city is Gomorrah, burning with the fire of lust, overindulgence and of ambition. Therefore its structures shall fall, and it shall be desolate and diminished; its inhabitants shall depart, and they shall groan in sorrow and tribulation, and they shall die out, and their shame shall be evident in many lands because I am angered at them."

Concerning the duke, who was privy to his brother's death, Christ speaks: "This man is full of pride. He boasts of his sins and cares nothing for what he has done to his neighbour. Therefore, if he does not humble himself, I will act in accordance with the common proverb: 'No lighter wails he who afterward weeps than he who wailed afore.' For he shall have a death no easier than his brother's—no, a death more bitter—unless he quickly amends himself."[59]

Concerning the duke's confessor, Christ speaks: "What did that friar say to you? Did he not say that the duke is good and cannot live in a better way? Did he not excuse the duke's sinfulness? Such men are not confessors but deceivers. They go about like simple sheep, but they are more truly foxes and flatterers. Such are those friends who see and propose 'assumptions and dejections' to human beings for the sake of some temporal reward. Therefore if that friar had stayed in his convent, he would have obtained less punishment and a greater crown. Now, however, he will not escape the hand of one who rebukes and afflicts."

Certain people advised the lady to change clothes and blacken her face and those of her companions because of the Saracens. Christ speaks: "What advice are they giving you? Is it not to disguise your clothes and blacken your faces? Would I, God, who instruct you, truly be like someone who does not know the future or like someone powerless who fears all things? Not in the least! But I am wisdom itself and power itself, and I foreknow all and can do all. Therefore retain your accustomed manner of clothing and your faces, and entrust your wills to me. For I,

---

[59]   Indeed, John was executed on the orders of Queen Eleanor in 1375.

who saved Sarah from the hands of her captors, will also save all of you on land and sea, and will provide for you in a way that is to your advantage."

Concerning a bishop, the Mother speaks: "My friend ought to love you as a mother, as a lady, as a daughter, and as a sister. As a mother, because of your age and because of the advice that he must seek. Second, as a lady, because of the grace given to you by God who, through you, has revealed the secrets of his wisdom. Third, as a daughter, by teaching and by consoling and by providing you with more useful things. Fourth, as a sister, by reproving—when this would be necessary—and by admonishing and by inspiring to greater things through word and example.

"Also, tell him that he ought to be like one who carries the most beautiful flowers. These flowers are my words, which are sweeter than honey to those who savour them, sharper and more penetrating than arrows. It is therefore the duty of the bearer to protect the flowers from the wind, the rain, and the heat: namely, from the wind of worldly talk; from the rain of carnal delights; from the heat of worldly favour. For one who glories in such things causes the flowers to become worthless and shows himself unsuitable to carry them."

Concerning the queen of Cyprus [Eleanor of Aragon (1333–1417)], the Son speaks: "Advise the queen not to return to her native land for it will not be to her advantage. But let her stay where she has been placed, serving God with all her heart. Second, she is not to marry, taking a second husband, for it is more acceptable to God to weep for the things that have been done and, by penance, to make up for time that has been uselessly spent. Third, she should guide the people of her kingdom toward mutual concord and charity; and she should labour that justice and good morals be upheld so that the community is not weighed down with heavy burdens. Fourth, for God's sake, she should forget the evils that were committed against her husband and not seek revenge. For I am the Judge, and I shall judge for her.

"Fifth, she should nurture her son with divine charity and appoint as his councillors men who are just and not covetous and, as members of his household, men who are modest, composed, and wise, from whom he may learn to fear God, to rule justly, to sympathize with the unfortunate, to flee from flatterers and sycophants, and to seek the advice of just men, even if they are poor, lowly or despised. Sixth, she is to ban the shameful custom of women wearing tight clothing which displays the breasts, the use of unguents, and many other vanities; for these are things displeasing to God.

"Seventh, she should find a confessor who, having left the world behind, loves souls more than gifts and neither glosses over sins nor fears to reprove them. And, in those things that pertain to the salvation of the soul, she is to obey him just as she obeys God. Eighth, she should seek out and be attentive to the lives of holy queens and saintly women; and she is to labour for the increase of God's honour. Ninth, she should be wise in giving gifts, avoiding both debt and the praises of men, for it is more acceptable to God to give a little or even nothing than to get into debt and to defraud one's neighbour."

On the crowning of the new king [Peter II, Eleanor's son], the Son speaks: "It is a great burden to be a king, but also a great honour and a very great pleasure. It is fitting, therefore, that a king be mature, experienced, prudent, just, and a hard worker who cares for his neighbours' welfare more than his own will. Therefore, in ancient times, kingdoms were well ruled when such a man was elected as king—one who had the will and the knowledge and the ability to rule with justice. Now kingdoms are not kingdoms but scenes of childishness, folly, and brigandage. For just as the brigand searches for ways and times to lay his ambush in order to steal money without being hurt, so kings now search for ways by which they can elevate their offspring, fill their purses with money, and discreetly burden their subjects. And they all the more gladly do justice in order to obtain temporal good, but they do not love justice in order to obtain everlasting reward.

"Therefore, a wise man said: 'Woe to that kingdom whose king is a child who lives well and is surrounded by flattery but cares nothing at all about the improvement of the community.' But because this boy will not bear his father's iniquity, therefore, if he wishes to make progress and to fulfil the dignity of his kingly name, let him obey my words that I have already spoken concerning Cyprus.

"And let him not imitate the behaviour of his predecessors, but let him lay aside childish levity and lead a kingly life, having strong ministers who do not love his gifts more than his soul and his honour, who hate flattery, and who are not afraid to speak the truth and to follow it and to assert it. Otherwise, the boy will have no joy in his people, and his people no joy in him."

Part 3: In the Holy Land

Book 7:70   Bridget receives instructions from the Virgin Mary about where she will stay in Jerusalem
Jerusalem, 1372

The mother speaks: "On the Mount of Zion there are two kinds of people. Some love God with all their heart. Others want God, but they love the world more. And therefore it is better to stay in the place intended for the pilgrims, which will encourage good things, so that the sluggish may be shaken from inertia and their descendants might follow their good example. For my Son will provide you with everything according to his will."

Book 7:14   Jesus declares to Bridget that her sins are forgiven
Jerusalem, Church of the Holy Sepulchre, 7 May 1372

The Son spoke to Bridget: "When you people entered my temple, which was dedicated with my blood, you were as cleansed of all your sins as if you had at that moment been lifted from the font of baptism. And because of your labours and devotion, some of your family's souls that were in purgatory have this day been liberated and have entered into heaven in my glory. For all who come to this place with a perfect will to amend their lives in accord with their better conscience, and who are unwilling to fall back into their former sins, will have all their former sins completely forgiven; and they will have an increase of grace to make progress."

Book 7:13   The devil disputes with the Virgin Mary and the guardian angel about the soul of Charles
Jerusalem, Church of the Holy Sepulchre, 7 May 1372

The Virgin Mary speaks to Lady Bridget and says: "I want to tell you what I did for the soul of your son Charles when it was being separated from his body. I acted like a midwife standing by a woman who is giving birth, to help the infant, lest it die in the flow of blood or suffocate in that narrow place through which an infant is born, and so that, through her watchful care, the infant's enemies, who are in the same house, will not be able to kill it. I acted in the same way for your son.

"Indeed, I stood near your son Charles, shortly before he died, in order that he might not have thoughts of carnal love in his memory and that, because of such thoughts, he would think or say anything against God or omit anything pleasing to God, or harm his soul by doing anything that could be in any way contrary to the divine will.

"I also helped him in that narrow space, i.e. his soul's exit from his body, so that in dying he would not suffer such great pain as to cause him to despair, and so that in dying he might not forget God. I also guarded his soul from its deadly enemies, i.e., the demons, so that none of them could touch it. As soon as his soul had left his body, I took custody of it and defended it, which quickly routed and dispersed the whole throng of demons who, in their malice, yearned to swallow it and torture it for eternity. But as to how, after the death of Charles, judgement was passed on his soul, this will be shown to you completely when it pleases me."

SECOND REVELATION ON THE SAME MATTER

After an interval of some days, the Virgin Mary herself again appeared to Lady Bridget, who was wide awake and at prayer, and said: "Through God's goodness, it is now permitted for you to see and hear how judgement was passed on the aforesaid soul when it had left the body. That which happened in one moment before God's incomprehensible majesty will be shown to you in great detail at intervals by means of corporeal likenesses so that your understanding may be able to grasp it."

In the same hour, therefore, Lady Bridget saw herself caught up to a certain large and beautiful palace where, upon the judgement seat, the Lord Jesus Christ sat as if crowned as an emperor in the company of an infinite host of attendant angels and saints. She saw standing near him his most worthy Mother, who listened carefully to the judgement. Also in the presence of the Judge, a soul was seen standing in great fear and panic, naked as a newborn infant, and, as it were, entirely blind so that it could see nothing; but it fully understood what was being said and done in the palace. An angel stood on the Judge's right side near the soul and a devil on his left. But neither of them touched the soul or handled it.

Then, at last, the devil cried out and said: "Hearken, O most almighty Judge! I complain in your sight about a woman who is both my Lady and your Mother and whom you love so much that you have given to her power over heaven and earth and over all of us demons of hell. She has indeed done me an injustice regarding that soul which now stands here. According to justice, as soon as this soul had left the body, I ought to have taken it to myself and presented it in my company before your court of judgement. And behold, O just Judge: that woman, your Mother, seized this soul with her own hands, almost before it exited from the man's mouth; and she has brought it to your judgement."

Then Mary, the Virgin Mother of God, answered thus: "Hearken, you devil, to my reply! When you were created, you understood the justice that was in God from eternity and without beginning or end. You also had free choice to do what most pleased you. And even though you have chosen to hate God rather than love him, nevertheless you still understand quite well what, according to justice, ought to be done. I tell you, therefore, that it was my business, rather than yours, to present that soul before God, the true judge.

"For while this soul was in the body it had a great love for me, and in its heart frequently pondered the fact that God had deigned to make me his mother and that he willed to exalt me on high above all created things. As a result, he began to love God with such a great love that in his heart he used to say this: 'I so rejoice because God holds the Virgin Mary his Mother most dear above all things, that there is in the world no creature and no bodily delight that I would take in exchange for that joy. No, I would prefer that joy to all earthly delights.

'And if it were possible that God could remove her, in the smallest point, from that dignity in which she stands, I would rather choose for myself, in exchange, eternal torture in the depth of hell. Therefore, to God himself be endless thanksgiving and everlasting glory for that blessed grace and that glory immeasurable that he has given to his most worthy Mother!' "Therefore, O devil, see now with what sort of will he passed away. Which now seems to you more just: that his soul come to God's judgement defended by me, or that it come into your hands to be tortured without pity?"

The devil answered: "I have no right to expect that this soul, which loves you more than itself, would come into my hands before judgement be passed. But even though, at the bidding of justice, you did him this favour before the judgement, nevertheless, after the judgement his works will condemn him to be punished at my hands. Now, O Queen, I ask you why you drove all of us demons from the presence of his body at his soul's exit so that none of us could cause any horror there or strike any fear into him?"

The Virgin Mary answered: "I did this in return for the ardent charity that he had toward my body and in return for the joy that he had from the fact that I am the Mother of God. Therefore I obtained from my Son the favour that, wherever he was and even where he now is, no evil spirit might approach his body."

After this, the devil speaks to the Judge and says: "I know that you are justice and power itself. You do not judge less justly for the devil than for an angel. Therefore adjudge that soul to me! Using the wisdom that I had when you created me, I had written down all his sins. Indeed, I had kept watch over all his sins with that malice that I had when I fell from heaven. For when that soul first came to the age of reason and really understood that what it was doing was sinful, its own will then drew it to live in worldly pride and carnal pleasure, rather than resist such things."

The angel answered: "When his mother first understood that his will was wavering toward sin, she immediately rushed to his aid with works of mercy and daily prayers that God might deign to have mercy on him lest he withdraw himself from God. Because of those works of his mother, he finally obtained a godly fear so that, as often as he fell into sin, he immediately hurried to make his confession."

The devil answered, "I must tell his sins." And at the very moment he intended to begin, he immediately started to exclaim and lament and carefully search himself, including his head and all the limbs that he seemed to have; and he was seen to tremble all over; and with great confusion he cried out: "Woe to me in my misery! How have I wasted my long labour? Not only is the text blotted out and ruined, but even the material on which everything was written has burnt up completely.

Moreover, the material indicates the times that he sinned. And I do not recall the times any more than the sins written down in connection with them."

The angel answered: "This was done by his mother's tears and long labours and many prayers. God sympathized with her sighs and gave to her son this grace: namely, that for every sin he committed, he obtained contrition, making a humble confession out of love for God. Therefore those sins have been blotted out and are unheeded by your memory."

The devil answered, asserting that he still had a sack full of those writings according to which the knight had resolved to make amends for his sins but did not take care [to do so and asserting that the writings gave grounds on which] to torture him until, through punishment, satisfaction had been made. And indeed that same knight had not yet taken care to amend those sins during his lifetime.

The angel answered: "Open the sack and seek a judgement on those sins for which you must chastise him." At those words, the devil cried out like a madman, saying: "I have been plundered in my power. Not only my sack has been taken, but also the sins that filled it! The sack in which I put all the reasons that I had to punish him was his laziness; for, because of his laziness, he omitted many good things."

The angel answered: "His mother's tears have plundered you and have burst the sack and have destroyed the writing. So greatly did her tears please God!"

The devil answered: "I still have here a few things to bring forth: namely, his venial sins."

The angel answered: "He had the intention to make a pilgrimage from his homeland, leaving his goods and his friends and visiting, by many labours, the holy places. He complemented these things, furthermore, by so preparing himself that he was worthy to gain an indulgence from Holy Church. Moreover, he desired, by making amends for his sins, to appease God his Creator. As a result, all those charges, which you just said that you had written down, have been pardoned."

The devil answered: "Nevertheless, I still must punish him for all those venial sins that he committed; and therefore, through indulgences, they have not been deleted at all. For there are thousands upon thousands of them, and they have all been written on my tongue."

The angel answered: "Extend your tongue and show the writing." The devil answered with loud howling and clamour like a maniac; and he said: "Woe is me. I have not one word to say; for my tongue has been cut off at the root together with its strength!"

The angel answered: "His mother did this with her continual prayers and her labour; for she loved his soul with her whole heart. Therefore, for the sake of her love, it pleased God to pardon all the venial sins that he committed from his infancy right up to his death; and therefore your tongue has lost its strength."

The devil answered: "I still have one thing carefully stored in my heart, and no one can abolish it. This thing is the fact that he acquired some things unjustly and never attended to their restoration."

The angel answered: "His mother made satisfaction for such things with her alms, her prayers, and her works of mercy so that the rigor of justice inclined toward the mildness of mercy; and God gave him the perfect intention of making full satisfaction—according to his opportunities and without sparing any of his own goods—to all those from whom he had taken anything unjustly. God accepted that intention in place of its effect because he was not well enough to live any longer. Therefore, his heirs must make satisfaction for such things to the extent that they can."

The devil answered: "If I therefore do not have the power to punish him for sins, I must nevertheless chastise him because he did not practise good deeds and virtues according to his ability while he had his full senses and a healthy body. For virtues and good deeds are those treasures that he ought to bring with him to such a kingdom, namely, to the glorious kingdom of God. Permit me therefore, by means of punishment, to supply what he lacks in virtuous deeds."

The angel answered: "It is written that, to one who asks, it shall be given and, to one who knocks with perseverance, it shall be opened. Listen then, you devil! By her charitable prayers and pious works his mother has perseveringly knocked at the gate of mercy on his behalf; and, for more than 30 years, she has shed many thousands of tears that God might deign to pour the Holy Spirit into his heart, so that this same son of hers might willingly offer his goods, his body and his soul to God's service. And God did so, for that knight became so fervent that it pleased him to live for nothing other than to follow God's will. And behold: God, who had been petitioned for so long a time, did pour his blessed Spirit into his heart.

"And the Virgin Mother of God has given to him, out of her own virtue, whatever he lacks in those spiritual weapons and garments that are proper for knights who must, in the kingdom of heaven, enter the presence of the highest Emperor. Those saints too, who now have a place in the heavenly kingdom and whom this knight loved during his life in the world, added to his consolation out of their merits. For he himself truly did assemble a treasure as those pilgrims do who daily exchange perishable goods for eternal riches.

"And because he did so, he will therefore obtain everlasting joy and honour, especially for his burning desire to make a pilgrimage to the holy city of Jerusalem, and for the fact that he fervently longed to risk his life willingly in warfare so that if he had been a match for so great a work, the Holy Land might be restored to the dominion of Christians, to the end that the glorious sepulchre of God might be held again in due reverence. Therefore you, O devil, have no right to speak of those things that he did not personally accomplish."

The devil answered: "Still, he lacks a crown. And if I could devise anything to spoil its perfection, I would willingly do so."

The angel answered: "It is entirely certain that all who will themselves from hell by truly repenting their sins, by voluntarily conforming themselves to the divine will, and by loving God himself with all their heart, will obtain his grace. And it pleases God himself to give them a crown out of the triumphal crown of his blessed human body if they have been purged according to strict justice. Therefore, it is not at all suitable for you, O devil, to devise anything related to his crown."

When the devil heard this, he cried out impatiently, roaring, and said: "Woe is me! For all my memory has been taken from me! I do not now recall in what respect that knight followed my will; and—what is more amazing—I have even forgotten what name he was called by while he lived."

The angel answered: "Know that now, in heaven, he is called 'Son of Tears.'" The devil cried out loudly and answered: "O, what a cursed sow his mother, that she-pig, is, who had a belly so expansive that so much water poured into her that her belly's every space was filled with liquid for tears! Cursed be she by me and by all my company!"

The angel answered: "Your curse is God's honour and the blessing of all his friends." Then, however, Christ the Judge spoke, saying this: "Depart, O devil, my enemy!" Then he said to the knight: "Come, O my chosen one!" And so, at once, the devil fled.

When Bridget saw these things, she said: "O Power eternal and incomprehensible, you yourself, God and Lord, Jesus Christ! You pour into hearts all good thoughts and prayers and tears. You conceal your gracious gifts; and for them you confer eternal rewards in glory. Therefore, to you be honour and service and thanks for all that you have created! O my sweetest God, you are most dear to me and truly to me dearer than my body and soul!"

The angel also then spoke to that same bride of Christ and said: "You ought to know that this vision has been shown to you by God not only for your own consolation but also in order that God's friends may be able to understand how much he deigns to do in answer to the prayers, tears, and labours of his friends who charitably pray and labour for others with perseverance and good will. You also ought to know that this knight, your son, would not have had such a grace if he had not, since infancy, had the will to love God and his friends and to amend his life willingly after every fall into sin."

Book 7:15   In a vision Bridget sees Jesus' suffering take place
Jerusalem, Church of the Holy Sepulchre, 7 May 1372

While I was at Mount Calvary, most mournfully weeping, I saw that my Lord, who was naked and scourged, had been led by the Romans to his crucifixion. He was being guarded by them diligently. I then saw too that a certain hole had been cut into the mount and that the crucifiers were there and ready to carry out their work. The Lord, however, turned toward me and said to me: "Be attentive; for in this hole in the rock the foot of the cross was fixed at the time of my passion." And at once I saw how the Romans were there fixing and fastening his cross firmly in the hole in the rock of the mount with bits of wood strongly hammered in on every side in order that the cross might stand more solidly and not fall.

Then, when the cross had been so solidly fastened there, at once wooden planks were fitted around the trunk of the cross to form steps up to the place where his feet were to be crucified, in order that both he and his crucifiers might be able to ascend by those plank steps and stand atop the planks in a way more convenient for crucifying him. After this, they then ascended by those steps, leading him with the greatest of mockery and scolding. He ascended gladly, like a meek lamb led to the slaughter. When he was finally on top of those planks, he at once, willingly and without coercion, extended his arm and opened his right hand and placed it on the cross. Those savage torturers pierced it with a nail through that part where the bone was more solid.

And then, with a rope, they pulled violently on his left hand and fastened it to the cross in the same manner. Finally, they extended his body on the cross beyond all measure; and placing one of his shins on top of the other, they fastened to the cross his feet, thus joined, with two nails. And they violently extended those glorious limbs so far on the cross that nearly all of his veins and sinews were bursting.

Then the crown of thorns, which they had removed from his head when he was being crucified, they now put back, fitting it onto his most holy head. It pricked his blessed head with such force that his eyes were filled with flowing blood and his ears were obstructed. And his face and beard were covered as if they had been dipped in that rose-red blood. And at once those crucifiers and soldiers quickly removed all the planks that abutted the cross, and then the cross remained alone and lofty, and my Lord was crucified upon it.

And as I, filled with sorrow, gazed at their cruelty, I then saw his most mournful Mother lying on the earth, as if trembling and half dead. She was being consoled by John and by those others, her sisters, who were then standing not far from the cross on its right side. Then the sorrow of the compassion of that most holy Mother so transfixed me that I felt, as it were, that a sharp sword of unbearable bitterness was piercing my heart. Then at last his sorrowful Mother arose; and in a state of physical exhaustion, she looked at her Son. Thus, supported by her sisters, she stood there dazed and overcome, as though dead yet living, transfixed by the sword of sorrow. When her Son saw her and his other friends weeping, with a tearful voice he commended her to John. It was quite discernible in his bearing and voice that out of compassion for his Mother, his own heart was also being penetrated by a most sharp arrow of sorrow beyond all measure.

Then too, his fine and lovely eyes appeared half dead; his mouth was open and bloody; his face was pale and sunken, all livid and stained with blood; and his whole body was as if black and blue and pale and very weak from the constant downward flow of blood. Indeed, his skin and the virginal flesh of his most holy body were so delicate and tender that, after the infliction of a slight blow, a black and blue mark appeared on the surface. At times, however, he tried to make stretching motions on the cross because of the intense and most acute pain that he felt. For at times the pain from his pierced limbs and veins ascended to his heart and battered him cruelly with an intense agony; and thus his suffering was prolonged amidst grave torment and great bitterness.

Then, therefore, in distress from the exceeding anguish of his pain and already near to death, he cried to the Father in a loud and tearful voice, saying: "O Father, why have you forsaken me?" He then had pale lips, a bloody tongue, and a sunken abdomen that adhered to his back as if he had no viscera within. A second time also, he cried out again in the greatest of pain and anxiety: "O Father, into your hands I commend my spirit." Then his head, raising itself a little, immediately bowed; and thus he sent forth his spirit. When his Mother saw these things, she trembled and would have fallen onto the earth if she had not been supported by the other women. Then, in that hour, his hands retracted slightly from the place of the nail holes because of the exceeding weight of his body; and thus his body was as if supported by the nails with which his feet had been crucified. Moreover, his fingers and hands and arms were now more extended than before; his shoulder blades and his back were pressed tightly to the cross.

Then the Jews standing around cried out in mockery against his Mother, saying many things. For some said: "Mary, now your Son is dead" and some said other mocking words. And while the crowds were watching, one man came running with the greatest of fury and pushed a lance in his right side with such violence and force that the lance would have passed almost through the other side of the body. Thus, when the lance was extracted from the body, at once a great stream, as it were, of blood spurted out; the iron blade of the lance and a part of the shaft came out of the body red and stained with the blood. Seeing these things, his Mother trembled violently and it was plain in her face and bearing that her soul was penetrated by the sharp sword of sorrow.

When all these things had been accomplished and when the large crowds were receding, certain of the Lord's friends took him down. Then, with pity, his Mother received him into her most holy arms; and sitting, she laid him on her knee, all torn as he was and wounded and black and blue. With tears, she and John and those others, the weeping women, washed him. And then his most mournful Mother wiped his whole body and its wounds with her linen cloth. And she closed his eyes and kissed them; and she wrapped him in a clean cloth of fine linen. And thus they escorted him with lamentation and very great sorrow and placed him in the sepulchre.

Book 4:70   The Virgin Mary describes Jesus' suffering
Italy, 1351 or later

The Mother speaks: "When my Son's passion was near at hand, tears filled his eyes and sweat covered his body from fear of suffering. Next, he was taken from my sight, and I did not see him again until he was led out to be scourged. He was then dragged along the ground and thrown down so cruelly and violently that it knocked his head about and broke his teeth. He was struck on his neck and cheek so forcefully that the sound of the blows reached my ears. At the command of the executioner, he undressed himself and freely hugged the pillar. He was bound with a rope and then scourged with barbed whips. The barbs caught in his skin and were then pulled backward, not just tearing but gouging him so as to wound his whole body.

"At the first blow, it was as though my heart had been pierced and I had lost the use of my senses. Then, coming out of it, I saw his whole wounded body—for his body was naked during the scourging. Then one of his enemies said to the executioners: 'Do you intend to kill this man without a sentence and cause his death yourselves?'

"He cut the ropes as he said this. Once released from the pillar, my Son turned first to get his clothes, but he was not given the time to put them on but was led away while still putting his arms into his sleeves. The footprints he left at the pillar were so full of blood that I could easily make them out and see which way they led. And he wiped his bloody face with his tunic.

"After the sentence, he was led out carrying the cross, but along the way another man took it from him. Once he arrived at the place of crucifixion, a hammer and four sharp nails were waiting there. He took off his clothes when ordered but covered his private parts with a small cloth. He proceeded to tie it on as though it gave him some consolation to do so.

"The cross was planted firmly, and the crossbeam was so placed that the junction of it was at the centre of his shoulder blades. The cross did not have any kind of headrest. The sign with his sentence on it was attached to each arm of the cross sticking out above the head.

"On being ordered, he lay down on the cross and, when he was asked to do so, first stretched out his right hand. Then, since his left hand could not reach the other corner of the cross, it had to be stretched out at full length. His feet were similarly stretched out to reach the slots for the nails and placed crosswise, and, as if they had been loosened from the shinbones, were fastened to the wood of the cross by two nails driven through solid bone, as had been done with his hands.

"At the first hammer stroke, I swooned away with sorrow, and when I awoke I saw my Son already fastened to the cross. I heard men saying to one another: 'What has this man committed—theft, robbery, or fraud?' Others answered that he was a fraud.

"Then the crown of thorns was pushed down on his head so hard that it came down to the middle of his forehead. Streams of blood poured down from where the thorns pierced him, filling his face and hair and eyes and beard so that almost nothing at all but blood could be seen. He could not even see me standing there by the cross without blinking to get rid of the blood.

"After he had entrusted me to his disciple, he lifted up his head, raised his weeping eyes to heaven, and cried out with a voice from deep within his chest, saying: 'My God, my God, why have you abandoned me?'

"Never was I able to forget that cry, not until I came to heaven, the cry that he uttered, moved more by my suffering than by his own.

"Now the colour of death appeared in those parts of his body that were visible beneath the blood. His cheeks were sunken. You could count his thin, naked ribs. His stomach, emptied now of all its juices, was sucked in toward his back, and even his nostrils looked pinched. When his heart was near to breaking, his whole body shook and his beard fell toward his chest.

"Just then, I collapsed lifeless to the ground.

"His mouth remained open, as he had already breathed his last. His tongue and teeth and the blood in his mouth were visible to those who were watching. His half-closed eyes had rolled backward. His now dead body sagged downward, with his knees bent to either side, and his feet bending on the nails like hinges.

"Meanwhile other people standing nearby said insultingly, 'O, Mary, your Son is dead.' Others, more noble minded, were saying: 'Lady, your Son's suffering is now ended unto his eternal glory.'

"A little later, after His side had been pierced, the lance was pulled out with blood that was brown in colour showing on its tip, which meant that the lance had pierced his heart. I felt that penetrating lance pierce my own heart, and it is a wonder that my heart did not burst.

"Though the others were going away, I could not go away. I felt almost comforted to be able to touch his body when it was taken down from the cross, and take it in my arms, and explore his wounds and wipe away the blood. I closed his mouth with my fingers and shut his eyes as well. I could not bend his rigid arms to repose on his chest but only across his stomach. His knees could not be straightened out but pointed outward in the same position in which they had stiffened on the cross."

The Mother speaks again: "Though you cannot see my Son as he exists in heaven, hear at least how he was in body on earth. He was so fair of face that no one, not even someone very sad at heart, could see him face-to-face without being cheered by the sight of him. The righteous were cheered with spiritual comfort, but even the wicked found relief from the sorrow of the world for as long as they looked on him. For that reason, people who were sad used to say: 'Let us go and see Mary's Son and at least find some relief as long as we are there.'

"In his twentieth year of age, he was perfect in height and manly strength, tall for the men of medium height in those days, not fleshy but well built in muscle and bone. His hair, eyelashes and beard were golden brown. His beard was a palm-width in length. His forehead was not sunken but straight. His nose was even, neither too little nor too large.

"His eyes were so limpid that even his enemies loved to gaze on him. His lips were not too thick and were bright red. His jaw did not jut out and was not too long, but attractive and of a fine length. His cheeks were nicely rounded. He was fair-skinned with traces of red, and he had a straight posture. There was not a blemish on his whole body, as his scourgers can testify who saw him bound to the pillar completely naked. There were never any lice or knots or dirt in His hair."

Book 6:94   The Virgin Mary reveals that she was the first to witness the resurrection of Jesus
Italy, late 1360s

The Mother of God speaks: "On such a day as this, my Son arose from the dead, strong as a lion, as he crushed the power of the devil and freed his chosen souls who ascended with him to the joy of heaven. But now you can ask where the souls he freed from the realm of death were before he ascended to heaven. I answer you that they were in a happy state that only my Son knew. For wherever my Son was and is, there is joy and glory. He said to the robber: 'Today you will be with me in paradise.' Many deceased saints also arose in Jerusalem; we saw them. Their souls ascended with my Son, but the bodies, together with the others, await judgement and resurrection. To me, who was the mother of God and who, after his death, was tormented by an indescribable grief, my Son appeared earlier than others; yes, he appeared to me physically, comforted me and reminded me that he would visibly ascend to heaven. And although this has not been written down for my humility's sake, it is still true that my resurrected Son has appeared to me sooner than anyone else."

Book 6:55   Mary tells how she was conceived and in the moment of the conception began salvation
Rome in 1350 or later when Bridget visited the relic chamber of the Basilica of San Paolo fuori le mura

The mother of God speaks: "When my father and my mother came together in marriage, they did this more by obedience than by will, and divine love here seemed more than the desire of the flesh. The moment when I was born may rightly be called a golden and precious moment, for other spouses come together by physical desire, but my parents came together in obedience to God's commandments. Yes, a golden moment was my birth, for then the salvation of all began and the darkness changed into light. For God wanted to do something unique and hidden from the world, as he does with the dry branch which becomes green. But know that my offspring was not known to all, for God desired that, like the law of nature and the voluntary choice between good and evil which preceded the written law, which would forbid all wrong intentions, God desired that his disciples would be doubtful concerning my offspring, and that each would show his piety, until the truth was revealed when the time was right."

Book 6:104   St Anna reveals a special prayer for obtaining offspring to married women

Rome in 1350 or later when Bridget visited the relic chamber of the Basilica of San Paolo fuori le mura

The Sacristan of St Paul's Outside the Walls of Rome gave Bridget relics of St Anna, Our Lady the Virgin Mary. When Bridget considered how she would keep and honour them, St Anna appeared to her and said, "I am Anna, the patroness of all true spouses in the old covenant. I am also the mother of all true believers in the new covenant, because God wanted to be born of my family. Therefore, you, my daughter, should honour God in this way: 'Blessed be you, Jesus, the Son of God and the Son of the Virgin, who have chosen you a mother of Anna and Joachim's marriage! Therefore, have mercy on Anna's prayers to all living in marriage, that they should bear fruit to God! Lead all those who intend to marry, that God may be honoured through them!' But my relics, which you have, will be a comfort to those who love them until God pleases them even more in the resurrection of the body."

Book 4:6   The apostle Paul talks about his participation in the stoning of Stephen, and of his conversion
Rome in 1350 or later when Bridget visited the relic chamber of the Basilica of San Paolo fuori le mura

St Paul speaks to Bridget saying: "My daughter, you compared me to a lion that was raised among wolves but was rescued from them in a wonderful way. I was indeed a greedy wolf, my daughter, but God made a lamb out of the wolf for two reasons. The first was because of his great love, for he makes the vessels of his grace out of unworthy materials, and he makes friends out of sinners. The second was because of the prayers of St Stephen, the first martyr.

"Let me describe how I was and what I had in mind at Stephen's stoning and why I deserved his prayers. I neither rejoiced nor delighted in St Stephen's sufferings, nor did I envy his glory. Still I wanted him to die because, to my mind, I did not see him as having the true faith.

"When I saw his great zeal and his patient endurance of suffering, I grieved terribly over his lack of faith—when in fact he was the truly faithful one and I altogether blind and faithless. Out of compassion for him I prayed and begged with my whole heart that his bitter sufferings might bring him to glory and reward. Because of this, his prayers benefited me first of all, for, through them, I was rescued from the many wolves and made into a gentle lamb.

"This is why it is good to pray for everyone, because the prayer of the righteous benefits those who are closer and better prepared to receive grace.

"However, I now complain that this man, who spoke so eloquently among the learned and was so patient before those who stoned him, has been wholly forgotten in the hearts of many people and especially neglected by those who ought to serve him night and day. They bring him their broken and empty vessels, dirty and repellent. Therefore, as it is written, they shall be clothed 'in double confusion and shame' and shall be thrown out of the houses of pleasure."

Book 1:9   Mary reveals her life and her role in salvation history
Sweden, sometime between 1344 and 1349

Mary speaks: "I am the Queen of Heaven. Love my Son, for he is most worthy; when you have him, you have all that is worthwhile. He is also most desirable; when you have him, you have all that is desirable. Love him, too, for he is most virtuous; when you have him, you have every virtue. I want to tell you how wonderful his love for my body and soul was and how much he honoured my name. My Son loved me before I loved him, since he is my Creator.

"He united my father and mother in a marriage so chaste that there could not be found a more chaste marriage at that time. They never wanted to come together except in accordance with the Law, and only then with the intention to bring forth offspring.

"When an angel revealed to them that Anna would give birth to the Virgin from whom the salvation of the world would come, they would rather have died than to come together in carnal love; lust was dead in them. I assure you that when they did come together, it was because of divine love and because of the angel's message, not out of carnal desire, but against their will and out of a holy love for God. In this way, my flesh was put together by their seed and through divine love. Then, when my body had been made and formed, God infused my created soul into it from his divinity, and my soul was immediately sanctified with my body, and the angels guarded and served it day and night. When my soul was sanctified and joined to my body, my mother felt such great joy that it would have been impossible to describe it!

"Afterwards, when my time on earth had been accomplished, my Son first raised up my soul—for it was the mistress of the body—to a more excellent place than others in heaven, close to his Divinity. Later, he also raised up my body in such a manner that no other creature's body is so close to God as mine. See how much my Son loved my soul and body! Yet there are some people with a malevolent spirit who deny that I was assumed into heaven, body and soul, and also others who simply do not know any better. But this is a most certain truth: I, with body and soul, was assumed to the Divinity!

"Hear now how much my Son honoured my name! My name is Mary, as it is said in the Gospel. When the angels hear this name, they rejoice and thank God for the great mercy that he worked through me and with me and because they see my Son's humanity glorified in his

Divinity. Those within the fire of purgatory rejoice exceedingly, just as a sick and bedridden man does if he receives a word of comfort that comforts his soul: he is suddenly overjoyed! When the good angels hear my name, they immediately move closer to the righteous for whom they are guardians and rejoice over their progress in good deeds and virtues.

"All humans have been given good angels for their protection, and bad angels to test them. The good angels are not separated from God; they serve the soul without leaving God. They are constantly in his sight. Yet they work to inspire the soul to do good. All the demons, however, shudder with fear at the name of Mary! When they hear the name, 'Mary', they immediately release a soul out of their claws. Just as a hawk, with its claws and beak embedded into its prey, releases it immediately if it is disturbed, but soon returns when it sees that there is no threat, so do the demons—frightened when they hear my name—release the soul. But they return and fly back as fast as an arrow if there is no improvement.

"No one is so cold in his love of God (unless he is damned) that he will not experience the devil releasing him from his habitual sins if only he invokes my name with the true intention of never returning to his evil deeds. The devil will never return to him unless he resumes his mortal sins. Sometimes, though, the devil is allowed to trouble him for the sake of his greater reward. However, the devil shall never own him."

Book 6:62   Mary talks about her death and assumption into heaven
Italy, after 1350

The Mother speaks: "When one day, a few years after my Son's ascension, I greatly desired to come home to my Son, I saw a radiant angel, as I had once seen, and he said to me: 'Your Son, who is our God and Lord, sent me to proclaim to you that the time is now come when you will come physically to receive the crown prepared for you.' I answered him, 'Do you know the day or the moment when I will leave this world?' The angel replied: 'Your Son's friends will come and bury your body.' Having said this, the angel disappeared, and I prepared for my passing, as I used to, by meditating on all the places where my Son had suffered. When one day my soul was uplifted by the wonder of God's love, my soul was filled with such joy that it could barely hold it, and in that moment my soul was separated from my body. But what wonderful things my soul saw then, and with what honour the Father and the Son and the Holy Spirit prepared it, lifted by a great number of angels, so many you would be unable to grasp, nor will I tell you until your soul and body are likewise separated, though I have shown you some of all this in the daily prayer that my Son has given you. But those who were with me in the house, when I gave up the spirit, understood by the strange light that filled the place what divine things then happened to me. Then, through divine prompting, my Son's friends were sent there, and buried my soul in the valley of Jehoshaphat, and with them were angels, as many as the rays of the sun, and the evil spirits did not dare approach. Fifteen days my buried body rested in the earth. Then it was assumed into heaven by a great multitude of angels . . . "

Book 1:8   Mary explains to Bridget how and why she should be praised
Sweden, sometime between 1344 and 1349

"I am the Queen of Heaven. You are concerned about how you should praise and honour me. Be certain that all praise of my Son also is praise of me, and those who dishonour him also dishonour me. This is so because I loved him and he loved me so ardently that both of us were like one heart. He so greatly honoured me, who was an earthen vessel, that he raised me above all the angels. Therefore, you should praise me like this:

'Blessed be you, God, creator of all things, who deigned to descend into the womb of the Virgin Mary! Blessed be you, God, who wished to be within the Virgin Mary without burdening her, and deigned to take immaculate flesh from her without sin! Blessed be you, God, who came to the Virgin, bringing joy to her soul and her whole body, and who left her body without sin, to the joy of her whole body! Blessed be you, God, who after your heavenly ascension gladdened the Virgin Mary, your Mother, with continuous comforts, and visited her with your consolation! Blessed be you, God, who assumed the body and soul of the Virgin Mary, your Mother, into heaven and honourably placed her above all the angels next to your divinity! Have mercy on me for the sake of all her prayers!'"

Book 7:26   The Virgin Mary confirms that she had been taken up to heaven
Jerusalem, 8 September 1372

When I was in the valley of Jehoshaphat, praying at the sepulchre of the glorious Virgin, that same Virgin appeared to me, shining with great splendour, and said: "Be attentive, daughter! After my Son ascended to heaven, I lived in the world for 15 years and as much time more as there is from the feast of the ascension of my Son until my death. And then I lay dead in the sepulchre for 15 days.

"Then I was assumed into heaven with great honour and joy. However, my garments in which I was buried remained in the sepulchre; and I was then clothed in such garments as those that clothe my Son and my Lord, Jesus Christ. Know also that there is no human body in heaven except the glorious body of my Son and my own body. Therefore go now, all of you, back to Christian lands; ever amend your lives for the better, and, in future, live with great care and attention now that you have visited these holy places, where my Son and I lived in the body and died and were buried."

Sermo Angelicus, Saturday's Reading 1: The angel tells how Mary took over the leadership
Rome, 1354

The angel speaks: "When Christ ascended to the glory of his kingdom, the Virgin Mary remained on earth. We cannot know what her presence meant to so many. Those who loved God were strengthened in their love; those who had turned from him were brought back to his love. The Apostles looked to her for guidance and counsel. The Martyrs found in her courage to face suffering and death. The Confessors of the Faith were strengthened in their belief. Virgins were drawn to her purity. Widows were consoled by her sorrows. Husbands and wives found in her a pattern of perfection. All who heard and obeyed the word of God found in Mary great comfort and help.

"Whenever the Apostles came to her, she was able to teach them about Christ, and help them to understand. The Martyrs rejoiced to suffer for Christ, for he had suffered for all. They remembered the long years of sorrow borne so patiently by Mary his Mother, and they bore their martyrdom even more readily. The Confessors, meditating on Mary, learnt many things about the truths of the Faith. From her example, they learnt too the wise use of earthly things: food, drink and sleep, work and rest, and how to order their lives in all things to the honour and glory of God.

"Virgins learnt from Mary's example true chastity in virtue. They learnt too the wise use of their time, how to avoid vanity and foolish talk, and see all things in the light of true holiness. From her widows learnt consolation in sorrow, strength against temptation, and humble submission to God's will. With a mother's love, Mary could never have wished for the death of her Son, still less for the death of the Son of God. Yet she willed in all things the will of God. For God's sake she chose the humble acceptance of suffering and sorrow.

Husbands and wives learnt from Mary true love for each other, in body and in soul, and the union of their wills, as of their flesh, in all that the will of God demanded. They learnt how she had united herself for ever with God by faith, and had never in any way shown resistance to his divine will."

Book 6:36   Jesus tells us how and why the Holy Spirit came

Jesus speaks: "I who speak to you are the same who sent my Holy Spirit to my apostles this day. He came to them in threefold ways: first as a stream, secondly as a fire, thirdly as tongues. He came to them through closed doors while they were alone and his coming had three good effects.

"First, they had a total desire to observe chastity and to live with restraint in every way.

"Second, they had a deep humility.

"Third, their whole longing was for God; they longed for nothing but God.

"They were like three clean and empty pots, and the Holy Spirit came and filled them. He came as a stream, for he filled all their joints and limbs with divine goodwill and comfort. He came as a fire, for the glow of divine love so lit their hearts that they loved and feared nothing but God.

"He came as tongues, for as the tongue is inside the mouth and yet does not damage the mouth but rather it helps a person to speak, so the Holy Spirit was inside their souls, helping them to long for nothing but me, and enabling them to speak with divine wisdom. By his power they spoke all truth. When those vessels were empty apart from divine longing, it was then that the Holy Spirit came to them. He cannot go to those who are already filled" (Acts Apostles 2:1–4).

Book 6:65 About the sisters in Bethany
The Son speaks: "You should also know that even though Mary's life is the best part, Martha's part is not wrong. On the contrary, it is commendable and pleasing to God. Therefore, I now want to tell you how Martha should be. Like Mary, she needs to have five good things.

"First, she must have the right faith of the Church of God.

"Second, she must know the commandments of God and the evangelical advisers, and perfect them in heart and deed.

"Third, she must restrain her tongue from every evil word that is against God and refrain from every inappropriate and unauthorized act, and guard the soul from excessive greed and desire. Furthermore, she should be satisfied with what has been given to her and not long for abundance.

"Fourth, she should, in a sensible and humble way, do merciful deeds that are pleasing to God.

"Fifth, she should love God above all things and more than herself. So did Martha, who gladly submitted herself to me by following me in words and deeds, and then, out of love for me, gave away all her belongings.

"For that reason, she felt distaste for earthly things and instead sought the heavenly. She patiently endured everything and cared for others before herself. She always thought of my love and suffering, rejoiced in her sorrows, and she loved everyone as a mother. This Martha followed me every day and wanted nothing more than to hear the words of life. She suffered with those who mourned, comforted the sick, cursed no one who wronged her, and prayed for everyone. Anyone who seeks love should follow Martha's example by loving his neighbour in order to inherit the kingdom of heaven, and not by adding to his burdens. One should imitate her by eschewing fame, pride and falseness. You should also not seek to make others envious.

"Notice that Martha, who prayed for her dead brother Lazarus, was the first to come to me, but her brother was not immediately raised. Then came Mary, and then their brother was raised by the prayer of both sisters. So it is in the spiritual life. Anyone who has an absolute desire to be a Mary should first be a Martha by doing physical work in my honour. She, or he, should know that s/he must first resist the desires of the flesh and resist the temptations of the devil. Therefore, s/he can contemplate ascending to Mary's position. For how can anyone who has not been tried and tempted and who has not triumphed over the flesh, be able constantly to hold on to the heavenly virtues? And who is Martha's and Mary's dead brother if not the imperfect deed? A good deed is often done without thought and with an indecisive mind and is therefore carried out in a lukewarm way. But in order for me to appreciate a good deed, it must be given new life through Martha and Mary's example. It happens when you genuinely love your neighbour for God's sake and above all, long for God. Then God appreciates every good deed of a person. That is why I said in the Gospel that Mary had chosen the better part. Martha's part is good when she mourns the sins of the people; her part is better when she considers how people can live wisely and honestly, and does so only for the love of God. But Mary's part is best when she is entirely focused on meditating about heavenly things and on what is good for people's souls. Then God ascends into the house of Martha and Mary, when the mind, filled with the good feelings of devotional love and freed from the world's troubles, always thinks of God as if he were present day and night and not only meditates but also meets God himself, enclosed in his love."

Book 4:72   Lazarus' awakening from death
Rome, after 1350.

The Son speaks: "There were two sisters, Martha and Mary, whose brother I raised from the dead. After his resurrection, he served me more than before. His sisters, too, though they had been my servants and cared greatly for me before their brother's resurrection, showed themselves as much more solicitous and devoted afterwards.

"I have treated you in a similar way spiritually. Thus, I raised your brother, that is, your soul that—decayed after being dead for four days—had separated itself from me by breaking my commandments, by unworthy desires, and by enjoyment of the world and of sin.

"There were, however, four reasons that moved me to raise Lazarus. The first was that he had been my friend while he lived. The second was the love of his sisters. The third was that Mary's humility had earned such a reward when she washed my feet. She deserved to be gladdened and honoured to the extent to which she had humbled herself for my sake before the guests. The fourth reason was to manifest the glory of my human nature.

"These four reasons do not, however, apply to you, since you love the world more than they did. Therefore, my mercy toward you is greater than my mercy toward those sisters. It is clearly all the greater, inasmuch as spiritual death is more dangerous than bodily death, and the resurrection of the soul is more glorious than bodily resurrection.

"Hence, since my mercy forgives your sins, welcome me, as those sisters did, into your minds with most fervent devotion, loving nothing as me, having total trust in me, each day humbling yourselves along with Mary by weeping for your sins, unashamed to live humbly among the proud, chaste among the unchaste, showing to others outwardly how much you love me. Furthermore, like those sisters, you ought to be of one heart and one mind, strong in scorning the world and quick to praise God. If you do so, then I will raise your brother—your soul—for you and protect it from being killed by the Jews.

"What would it have profited Lazarus to rise from death, unless, by living more virtuously in the present life, he might rise up more glorious to a second and lasting life? Who were the Jews who sought to kill Lazarus if not those who became indignant because he led better lives than theirs, who learned to speak loftily but to do little, who, seeking the approval of others, scorned the deeds of their predecessors with all the greater scorn the less they themselves deign to understand the higher truths?

"There are many such people. They know how to talk about virtues but not to live by them. Their souls are therefore in danger, because their words are many, but their deeds are nowhere to be seen. Did my disciples act in this manner? By no means! They did not admonish sinners with lofty words but with few and charitable words, and they were ready to give their own souls for those of sinners. Through their charity, others obtained charity, for the teacher's zeal informs the listener more than mere words do. Many preachers nowadays say abstruse things about me, but no fruit comes of it; wood is not set alight by merely blowing on it but only with the aid of sparks of fire.

"I shall guard and protect you from these Jews so that you will not leave me because of what they do or say. Yet I shall not protect you in such a way that you escape every suffering, but that you may not succumb through a lack of patient endurance. Stick to your resolution, and I shall strengthen your will with my love."

Book 3:11   John the Baptist explains how the rich can enter the kingdom of heaven
Rome, during the Jubilee year 1350

John the Baptist speaks: "The One who appears to you is the very Son of God, whom I myself heard the Father bear witness to when he said: 'This is my Son.' From him proceeds the Holy Spirit who appeared above him in the form of a dove as I was baptizing him. He is the Son of the Virgin according to the flesh. I touched his body with my very own hands.

"Believe firmly in him and enter into his life. He is the One who has shown the true path by which poor and rich can enter heaven. But you might ask, what should the character of a rich person be if he is to enter heaven, given that Jesus himself said that it is easier for a camel to go through the eye of a needle than for a rich man to enter heaven?

"To this I answer you: a rich man whose wealth is not acquired by dishonourable means, who is concerned not to spend his wealth wastefully or contrary to God's will, who holds his possessions and status with reluctance and would willingly be separated from them, who is disturbed by the loss of souls and the dishonour done to God, and, although his position in the world is God's will for him, he is vigilant to express God's love in his every deed, this is the kind of rich man who bears fruit and is dear to God."

Book 7:21   The Virgin Mary fulfils her promise and shows Bridget how Jesus was born
Bethlehem, August 1372

When I was at the manger of the Lord in Bethlehem, I saw a Virgin, pregnant and very beautiful, clothed in a white mantle and a finely woven tunic through which I could clearly discern her virginal flesh. Her womb was much swollen, for she was now ready to give birth. With her there was a very dignified old man; and they had both an ox and an ass with them. When they had entered the cave, and after the ox and the ass had been tied to the manger, the old man went outside and brought to the Virgin a lighted candle and fixed it in the wall and went outside in order not to be personally present at the birth.

And so the Virgin took the shoes from her feet and the white mantle that covered her, and removed the veil from her head, and laid these things beside her, remaining in only her tunic, with her beautiful hair—as if of gold—spread out upon her shoulder blades. She then drew out two small cloths of linen and two of wool, very clean and finely woven, which she carried with her to wrap the infant that was to be born, and two other small linens to cover and bind his head; and she laid these cloths beside her so that they were ready to use.

And when all these things had thus been prepared, then the Virgin knelt with great reverence to pray; and she kept her back toward the manger and her face toward the east, lifted up to heaven. And so, with raised hands and with her eyes intent on heaven, she was as if suspended in an ecstasy of contemplation, full of divine sweetness. And while she was thus in prayer, I saw the One lying in her womb then move; and then and there, in a moment and the twinkling of an eye, she gave birth to a Son, from whom there went out such great and ineffable light and splendour that the sun could not be compared to it. Nor did the candle that the old man had put in place give any light, because it was eclipsed by the light of divine splendour.

So sudden and momentary was the moment of birth that I was unable to discern how it had happened. But yet, at once, I saw that glorious infant lying on the earth, naked and glowing with light. His flesh was clean. I saw also the afterbirth, lying wrapped very neatly beside him. And then I heard the wonderfully sweet songs of the angels. And the Virgin's womb, which before the birth had been very swollen, at once retracted; and her body looked wonderfully beautiful and delicate.

When therefore the Virgin knew that she had given birth, at once she bowed her head and joined her hands, and with great dignity and reverence she adored the child and said to him: "Welcome, my God, my Lord, and my Son!" And then the boy, crying and, as it were, trembling from the cold and the hardness of the pavement where he lay, rolled a little and extended his limbs, seeking to find refreshment and his Mother's love. Then his Mother took him in her hands and pressed him to her breast, and with cheek and breast she warmed him with great joy and tender maternal compassion.

Then, sitting on the earth, she put her Son in her lap and deftly caught his umbilical cord with her fingers. At once it was cut off, and no liquid or blood flowed from it. And she began to wrap him carefully, first in linen cloths and then in woollen ones, binding his little body, legs and arms with a ribbon that had been sewn into four parts of the outer woollen cloth. And afterwards she wrapped and tied on the boy's head the two small linen cloths that she had prepared for this purpose.

When these things were accomplished, the old man entered; and prostrating himself on the earth, he adored him on bended knee and wept for joy. The Virgin was unaffected by the birth; her bodily strength was not depleted, as is the case in other women giving birth. Only her swollen womb retracted to its normal size, as it had been before she conceived. Then, she arose, holding the boy in her arms; and together she and Joseph put him in the manger, and on bended knee they continued to adore him with gladness and immense joy.

Book 7:22   The Virgin Mary confirms the previous revelation
Bethlehem, August 1372

Afterwards again in the same place, the Virgin Mary appeared to me and said: "My daughter, it is a long time ago that I promised you in Rome that I would show to you here in Bethlehem the manner of my childbearing. And even though I showed to you in Naples something about this—namely, what state I was in when I gave birth to my Son—nevertheless, know for certain that I gave birth in such a manner as you have now seen: on bended knee, praying alone in the stable. I gave birth to him with such great exultation and joy of soul that I felt no discomfort when he left my body, and no pain. But at once I wrapped him in the small clean cloths that I had prepared before.

When Joseph saw these things, he marvelled with great gladness and joy because I had given birth without help. But because the great multitude of people in Bethlehem was busy about the census, they were therefore so attentive to it that the wonders of God could not be published among them. And therefore it is the truth that, however much human beings, following their human perception, try to assert that my Son was born in the common manner, it is nevertheless true and beyond any doubt that he was born just as I told you and just as you now have seen."

Book 7:23   In a vision in the birth cave Bridget sees when the shepherds came to worship Jesus
Bethlehem, August 1372

I saw also in the same place, while the Virgin Mary and Joseph were adoring the boy in the manger, that shepherds and guardians of the flock then came to see and adore the infant. When they had seen it, they first wished to inquire whether it were male or female, because the angels announced to them that the Saviour of the world had been born and had not said "savioress". Therefore the Virgin Mother then showed to them the infant's natural parts and male sex; and at once they adored him with great reverence and joy; and afterward they returned praising and glorifying God for all these things that they had heard and seen.

Book 7:24   In a vision of the birth cave the Virgin Mary speaks about the wise men's visit
Bethlehem, August 1372

The same Mother of the Lord also said to me: "My daughter, know that when the three magi kings came into the stable to adore my Son, I had foreknown their coming well in advance. And when they entered and adored him, then my Son exulted, and for joy he had then a more cheerful face. I too rejoiced exceedingly; and I was gladdened by the wonderful joy of exultation in my mind, while being attentive to their words and actions, keeping those things and reflecting on them in my heart."

Part 4: Home from the Holy Land

Book 7:20   Jesus answers the Franciscan friar Martin of Aragon's questions he posed to Bridget
Bethlehem, August 1372

Infinite thanksgiving and humble service, praise, and honour be to God in his power and everlasting majesty—to him who is one God in three persons! It pleased his immense goodness to speak to a person at prayer, saying this: "Hear, O you to whom it has been given to hear and see spiritual things; and diligently hold in your memory these my words. There was a man named Francis. When he turned away from worldly pride and covetousness and from the flawed delight of the flesh and turned toward a spiritual life of penance and perfection, he then obtained true contrition for all his sins and a perfect intention of amendment, saying: 'There is nothing in this world that I am not willing to give up gladly for the sake of the love and honour of my Lord Jesus Christ. There is also nothing so hard in this life that I am not willing to endure it with gladness because of his love, doing all that I can for the sake of his honour, according to my strength in body and soul. And I want to lead and strengthen all others that I can, so that they love God above all with the whole of their heart.'

"The Rule of this Francis, which he himself began, was not dictated and composed by his human understanding and prudence, but by me in accordance with my will. For every word that is written in it was breathed into him by my Spirit; and afterwards, he gave that Rule to others. So too, all other Rules that my friends began and themselves personally kept and observed and effectively taught and gave to others were not dictated and composed by their own understanding and human wisdom, but by the indwelling of that same Holy Spirit. For a number of years, the brothers of this Francis—who are called Friars Minor—held and kept that Rule well, both spiritually and devoutly, in whole accordance with my will.

"As a result, the devil, the ancient fiend, felt great envy and unrest because he had not the strength to conquer the friars by his temptations and deceits. Therefore, the devil sought diligently that he might find a man whose human will he could join together with his own malign spirit. At last, he found a cleric who thought thus: 'I would like to be in a position where I could have worldly honour and bodily pleasure, and where I could amass so much money that I would lack nothing at all for my needs and pleasures. Therefore, I will enter the Order of Francis; and I will pretend to be very humble and obedient.' And so, with that intention and will, the aforementioned cleric entered the said order; and at once the devil entered into his heart. And thus the said cleric became a friar in the said order.

"Inwardly, however, the devil considered in this manner: 'Just as Francis, with his humble obedience, wishes to draw many from the world to receive great rewards in heaven, so this my friar—who will be named "Adversary" because he will be the adversary of the Rule of Francis—will draw many in the Order of Francis from humility to pride, from poverty to covetousness, from true obedience to the doing of one's own will and to the pursuit of bodily pleasure.'

"And when the aforesaid Brother Adversary entered the Order of Francis, at once, at the devil's instigation, he began to think inwardly thus: 'I will show myself so humble and obedient that all will reckon me a saint. When the others are fasting and keeping silence, then I, with special companions, shall do the contrary: namely, by eating and drinking and talking so secretly that none of the others will know or understand. Also, according to the said Rule, I cannot lawfully touch money or possess gold or silver; therefore I will have some special friend to keep my money and gold secretly on my behalf so that I may use that money as I will.

'I also want to learn the liberal arts and science, so that from them I may be able to have some honour and dignity in the order, having horses and silver vessels and handsome clothes and costly ornaments. And if anyone reproves me for these things, I shall answer that I do it for the honour of my order, if besides, I could work further and do so much that I would be made a bishop, then I would truly be happy and blessed in such a life as I then could lead, for then I would enjoy my personal freedom and I would have all my bodily pleasures.'

"Now hear what the devil had done in the aforesaid Order of Francis. For it is true that in the world the friars who, either in action or desire, hold the aforesaid Rule that the devil taught to Brother Adversary, are more numerous than those who keep the Rule that I myself taught to Brother Francis. You should nevertheless know that however much those friars—namely, those of Francis and those of Brother Adversary—live together in the world, I will nevertheless separate them after death, for I am their Judge. Those friars who faithfully follow the Rule of Francis are to remain with me, together with Francis, in everlasting joy. But those who belong to Brother Adversary's Rule will be doomed to eternal punishments in the depth of hell if before death they will not correct themselves and humbly amend their lives.

"Nor is this to be wondered at, for those who ought to be examples of humility and sanctity to worldly human beings are actually vile and ribald examples through their pride and covetousness. And therefore both the said friars themselves and all other religious who are prohibited from having private property and yet have property, against their Rule, and who wish to appease me by conferring upon me a part of it, should know for certain that their gifts are abominable to me and hateful and unworthy of any good gift in return. For it is more agreeable and pleasing to me that they diligently observe the blessed poverty that they professed according to their Rules, than that they might present to me all the gold and silver in the world.

"You, O woman who hear my words, should also know that it would not have been permitted for you to know this afore-spoken vision if it had not been for a good servant of mine who sincerely petitioned me with all his heart on behalf of that Friar Minor, and who, out of divine charity, desired to give to that same friar some advice useful to his soul."

When these things had been seen and heard, this vision disappeared.

Book 7:18   In Jerusalem, Bridget gives advice to the queen of Cyprus about the king and his uncle
Jerusalem, summer 1372

The bride writes to the king of Cyprus and to the prince of Antioch: "The first counsel is that each of you, in the presence of his confessor, is to make a clean and complete confession of all the things that he has done against the will of God; and thus you are to receive the blessed Body of our Lord Jesus Christ with fear and love of God. The second counsel is that both of you are to be united in true love so that you may be one heart toward God and his honour, ruling the kingdom for the honour of God and the good of your subjects.

"The third counsel is that both of you are to be united in true charity with your subjects and that, solely out of reverence for the passion and death of Jesus Christ, you are to forgive and spare all who, by advice, deed, or approbation, cooperated in the death of your father King Peter. Offer them your charity with all your heart, in order that God may include you in his mercy and also that he will strengthen you to rule the kingdom for his honour.

"The fourth counsel is that, since divine providence has appointed you the governors of the kingdom, you should use all possible diligence in speaking to all the prelates, both of the churches and of the religious orders, effectively but charitably advising them that they and their subjects should all correct themselves in all those matters from which they have deviated, either spiritually or temporally, from the holy state of their predecessors of earlier times, and that they should quickly return to live purely in holiness so that their lives may be totally reformed. Then they and their subjects, having truly amended their lives, may obtain God's friendship and be made worthy to pray that God may mercifully renew in holiness the universal Church.

"The fifth counsel is that, for the sake of that great love which God has for your souls, you should also love the souls of your subjects, advising your military people that all who have in any way offended God should quickly and humbly correct themselves, and that all who are under obedience to the Roman Church and who have reached the age of reason should humbly exercise the practice of confession; that they should reconcile themselves to those neighbours they have offended and establish a concord with them; and that, having amended their lives, they should humbly receive the Body of Christ.

"Thereafter, they are to lead a Catholic life: namely, living faithfully in marriage or in widowhood or in the state of praiseworthy virginity; observing all that Holy Church teaches; leading, with loving hearts, the members of their household and their servants and their subjects and all others possible, by their good example and by word and deed, to do the same; and strengthening those in such states by their good admonitions. And know for certain that all who are not willing to obey in these matters will suffer the cost in body and soul.

"The sixth counsel is that you should tell all prelates that they must effectively and frequently admonish all their clerics, namely, the rectors of churches; that each of them is to inquire diligently in his parish whether there be any of his parishioners who persist in living sinful lives, causing offence to God and contempt for Holy Mother Church.

"Any such people who are found thus are to be warned of the peril to their souls; and they are to teach them such measures and spiritual practices by which they can and must humbly amend their lives. If, however, some of those who live in sinful lives will not humbly obey, then the same rectors must not delay in reporting to their superiors and the bishops in order that the prelates may correct the stubbornness of such obstinate persons by means of an ecclesiastical censure.

"If, because of the sinners' stubbornness and pride or because of their temporal power, the aforesaid bishops and prelates are unable to correct or punish them, then you, my lords, are advised to be, with the power available to you, workers with the lord prelates so that by your help sinners may be brought to correction, so that, having amended their lives, they may attain God's mercy."

Book 7:19   Revelation on Cyprus and its future
Received in Jerusalem, summer 1372

When Bridget was wide awake and absorbed in prayer she became suspended in an ecstasy of contemplation, and she saw herself caught up in spirit to a palace that was of incomprehensible size and indescribable beauty. And it seemed to her that Jesus Christ was sitting among his saints on the imperial seat of majesty. He opened his blessed mouth and uttered these words that are noted below:

"I truly am supreme charity itself; for all things that I have done from eternity, I have done out of charity; and, in the same way, all things that I do and shall do in the future proceed entirely from my charity. For charity is as incomprehensible and intense in me now as it was at the time of my passion when, through my death and from exceeding charity, I freed from hell all the elect who were worthy of redemption and liberation. For if it were still possible that I might die as many times as there are souls in hell so that for each of them I might again endure such a death as I then endured, my body would still be ready to undergo all these things with a glad will and most perfect charity. But it is now impossible that my body could once more die or suffer any pain or tribulation. And it is also impossible that any soul that, after my death, has been or will be condemned to hell would ever again be freed from there, or would enjoy the heavenly gladness that my saints and chosen ones enjoy at the glorious sight of my body.

No, the damned will feel the pains of hell in an everlasting death because they did not choose to be saved by my death and passion and did not follow my will while they lived in the world. However, because no one is judge over the offences done to me except myself, and, for this reason, the charity that I have shown to human beings is judged according to my will.

"Now I make my complaint about the inhabitants of the kingdom of Cyprus as if they were one human being. But I do not complain about my friends who dwell there and who love me with all their heart and follow my will in all things; but I speak in complaint, as if to one person, to all those who scorn me, resist my will and greatly oppose me.

"O people of Cyprus, my adversary, listen and be diligently attentive to what I say to you! I have loved you as a father loves his only son, whom he has willed to exalt to all honour. I conferred on you a land in which you could have in abundance all things necessary for the sustenance of your body. I sent to you the warmth and light of the Holy Spirit that you might understand the right Christian faith to which you faithfully bound yourself, humbly subjugating yourself to the sacred statutes and to the obedience of Holy Church.

"Indeed, I gave you a place that would be fitting for a faithful servant, namely, among my enemies, so that in return for your earthly labours and for the physical struggle of battles you would obtain in my heavenly kingdom an even more precious crown. I also carried you for a long time in my heart, i.e., in the charity of my Godhead, and kept you as the apple of my eye in all your adversities and tribulations. And as long as you observed my precepts and were faithful to the statutes of Holy Church, then certainly many souls come from the kingdom of Cyprus to my heavenly kingdom, to enjoy eternal glory with me for ever.

"But because you now follow your own will and all those things that delight your heart, without fearing me who am your Judge and without loving me who am your Creator and who also redeemed you through my death; and because you spat me out of your mouth like some foul and unsavoury thing; and, indeed, because you have enclosed the devil together with your soul in the chamber of your heart; and because you have driven me thence as if I were a thief and a robber; and because you were no more ashamed to sin in my sight than animals are in their mating, it is therefore a fitting justice and a just judgement that you should be driven out from all my friends in heaven and be placed forever in hell amidst my enemies.

"And know this without a doubt: that my Father—who is in me, and I am in him, and the Holy Spirit is in us both—is himself my witness that nothing but truth has ever left my mouth. Wherefore, know as truth that if anyone has been so disposed as you now are, and if he will not amend his life, his soul will go the same way as Lucifer's because of his pride, and Judas, who betrayed me because of his greed, and Zimri, whom Phinehas killed because of his lust. For Zimri sinned with a woman against my law; and therefore, after his death, his soul was condemned to hell.

"Wherefore, O people of Cyprus, I now announce to you that if you will not correct yourself and amend your life, then I shall so destroy your generation and progeny in the kingdom of Cyprus that I shall spare neither the poor person nor the rich. Indeed, I shall so destroy this same generation of yours that in a short time, the memory of you will disappear from the hearts of human beings as if you had never been born in this world. Afterward, however, it is my pleasure to plant new plants in this kingdom of Cyprus that will carry out my precepts and will love me with all their heart.

"Nevertheless, know for a certainty that if any one of you wills to correct himself, amend his life, and humbly turn back to me then, like a loving shepherd, I shall joyfully run out to meet him, lift him onto my shoulders and carry him back to my sheep. If anyone amends his life, he will share in the benefit of my passion and death, and he will receive with me eternal consolation in the kingdom of heaven.

"You should also know for certain that you, my enemies who dwell in this said kingdom, were not worthy that such a vision or divine revelation should be sent to you. But some friends of mine who live in the same kingdom and faithfully serve me and love me with their whole heart have, by their labours and tearful prayers, inclined me to make you understand, by means of this my revelation, the grave peril of your souls. For to some of my friends there, it has been divinely shown by me how many countless souls from this said kingdom of Cyprus are being excluded from heavenly glory and are being eternally doomed to the death of Gehenna.

"However, the above words I speak to those Latin Christians subject to the obedience of the Roman Church, and who, at baptism, vowed to me to live in the Roman Catholic faith, and who, through works contrary to me, have totally withdrawn from me. Greeks, however, who know that all Christians must hold only one Catholic Christian faith and be obedient to the Roman Catholic Church, and have, as spiritual pastor over them, only my sole vicar general in the world, the supreme Roman pontiff, and who, nevertheless, will not spiritually subject and humbly subjugate themselves to that same Roman Church and to its head, through stubborn pride, greed or wantonness of the flesh or some other worldly thing, are unworthy to obtain pardon and mercy from me after death.

"But the other Greeks, who would desire to know the Roman Catholic faith, but cannot, and who nevertheless, if they knew it and had the ability, would willingly and devoutly receive it and would humbly subjugate themselves to it and who, nonetheless, following their conscience, do abstain from sin and live piously—to such as these, after their death, I will be merciful when they are called to my judgement.

"The Greeks should also know that their empire and kingdoms or domains will never be secure and peaceful, but that they themselves will always be subject to their enemies from whom they will always sustain the gravest of losses and daily miseries until, with true humility and charity, they devoutly subject themselves to the Church and faith of Rome, totally conforming themselves to the sacred constitutions and rites of that same Church."

When these things had been seen and heard in spirit, the vision disappeared; and Bridget remained at prayer, full of awe and wonder.

Book 7:27   Christ complains about the Neapolitan women's make-up and dress
Naples, in February 1373

To Bridget, who was wide awake at prayer and absorbed in contemplation, Jesus Christ appeared; and he said to her this: "Hear, O you to whom it has been given to hear and see spiritual things; and be diligently attentive; and in your mind beware in regard to those things that you now will hear and that on my behalf you will announce to the nations, lest you speak them to acquire for yourself honour or human praise. Nor indeed are you to be silent about these things from any fear of human reproach and contempt; for these things that you are now going to hear are being shown to you not only for your own sake, but also because of the prayers of my friends.

"For some of my chosen friends in Naples have for many years asked me with their whole heart—in their prayers and in their labours on behalf of my enemies living in the same city—to show them grace through which they could be saved from their sins and abuses. Swayed by their prayers, I give to you now these words of mine; and therefore diligently hear the things that I speak.

"I am the Creator of all and Lord over both angels and devils, and no one will escape my judgement. The devil, in fact, sinned in three ways against me: through pride; through envy; and through arrogance, i.e., through love of his own will. He was so proud that he wanted to be lord over me and that I should be subject to him. He envied me so much that if it were possible he would gladly have killed me in order to be lord himself and sit on my throne. Indeed, his own will was so important to him that he cared nothing at all about my will. Because of this, he fell from heaven and, no longer an angel, he became a devil in the depth of hell.

"Afterward, however, seeing the malice and envy that he had toward humankind, I revealed my will and gave my commandments to human beings that by doing them they could please me and displease the devil. Finally, because of the charity that I have toward human beings, I came into the world and was born of a virgin. Indeed, I personally taught human beings the true way of salvation by work and by word; and to show them perfect charity and love, I opened heaven for them by my own blood.

"But what are my enemies among human beings doing to me now? In truth, they have contempt for my precepts; they cast me out of their hearts like a loathsome poison; indeed, they spit me out of their mouths like something rotten; and they abhor the sight of me as if I were a leper in the worst stages of decay. But the devil and his works they embrace in their every affection and deed. For they bring him into their hearts, doing his will with delight and gladness and following his evil suggestions. Therefore, by my just judgement they shall have their reward in hell with the devil eternally without end.

"For in place of their pride, they will have confusion and eternal shame to such a degree that angels and demons will say of them: 'They are filled with confusion to the very utmost!' And for their insatiable greed, each devil in hell will so fill them with his deadly venom that no part of their souls will remain unfilled with diabolic venom. And for the lust with which they burn like senseless animals, they will never see my face but will be separated from me and deprived of their will.

"Moreover, know that just as all mortal sins are very serious, so too a venial sin is made mortal if a human being delights and continues in it. Wherefore, know that two sins, which I now name to you, are being practised and that they result in other sins that could be thought of as venial. But because the people delight in them and intend to continue in them, they are therefore made mortal, and the people in the city of Naples commit many other abominable sins that I do not wish to name to you.

"The first of the two sins is that rational human creatures are painting their faces with the various colours with which insensible images and statues of idols are coloured, so that to others, their faces may seem more beautiful than when I made them. The second sin is that the bodies of men and women are being deformed from their natural state by unseemly forms of clothing. And the people are doing this because of pride and so that, in their bodies, they may seem more beautiful and more lascivious than when I, God, created them. And they do this so that those who see them thus may be quickly provoked and inflamed toward carnal desire. Therefore, know for certain that as often as they daub their faces with antimony and other extraneous colouring, some of the infusion of the Holy Spirit is diminished in them and the devil draws nearer to them. In fact, as often as they adorn themselves in disorderly and indecent clothing and so deform their bodies, the adornment of their souls is diminished and the devil's power is increased.

"O my enemies, who do such things and with effrontery commit other sins contrary to my will, why have you neglected my passion; and why do you not attend in your hearts to how I stood bound and naked at the pillar, cruelly scourged with hard whips, and to how I was nailed naked on the cross and cried out, wounded and covered in blood? And when you paint and anoint your faces, why do you not look at my face and see how it was full of blood? You are not even attentive to my eyes, how they grew dark and were covered with blood and tears, and how my eyelids turned blue.

"Why too do you not look at my mouth or gaze at my ears and my beard and see how they were torn and stained with blood? You do not look at the rest of my limbs, grievously wounded by torture, and see how I hung black and blue on the cross and died for your sake. And there, derided and rejected, I was despised by all in order that, by recalling these things and attentively remembering them, you might love me, your God, and thus escape the devil's snares, in which you have been horribly bound.

"However, in your eyes and hearts, all these things have been forgotten and neglected. And so you behave like prostitutes, who love the pleasure and delight of the flesh, but not its offspring. For when women feel a living infant in their womb, at once they procure an abortion by herbs and other means, so that they may continue in their lust and carnal pleasure. This is how you behave. For I, God, your Creator and Redeemer, visit all with my grace, knocking, namely, at your hearts, because I love all.

"But when you feel, in your hearts, any inpouring—namely of my Spirit—or any compunction; or when, through hearing my words, you conceive any good intention, at once you procure spiritually, as it were, an abortion: you excuse your sins and delight in them and are even determined to continue in them. Instead you do the devil's will, putting him in your hearts and expelling me in this contemptible way. Therefore, you are without me, and I am not with you. And you are not in me but in the devil, for it is his will and his suggestions that you obey.

"And so, because I have just spoken my judgement, I shall also now speak my mercy. My mercy, however, is this: namely, that none of my enemies is so strong or so great a sinner that my mercy would be denied him if he were to ask for it humbly and wholeheartedly. Wherefore, my enemies must do three things if they wish to reconcile themselves to my grace and friendship. The first is that with all their heart they repent and have contrition because they have offended me, their Creator and Redeemer. The second thing is confession—clean, frequent and humble—which they must make before their confessor.

"And thus let them amend all their sins by doing penance and making satisfaction in accord with that same confessor's counsel and discretion. For then I shall draw close to them, and the devil will be kept far away from them. The third thing is that, after they have thus performed these things with devotion and perfect charity, they are to go to Communion and receive and consume my Body, with the intention of never falling back into former sins but of persevering in good practices, even to the end.

"If anyone, therefore, amends his life in this manner, at once I will run out to meet him as a loving father runs to meet his wayward son; and I will receive him into my grace more gladly than he himself could have asked or thought. And then I will be in him, and he in me; and he shall live with me and rejoice forever. But upon him who continues in his sins and malice my justice shall undoubtedly come. For when the fisherman sees the fish in the water in their delight and merriment, even then he drops his hook into the sea and draws out the fish, then putting it to death—not all the fish at once, but a few at a time—until he has taken them all.

"This is indeed what I shall do to my enemies who continue in sin. For I shall bring them a few at a time to the end of their earthly lives, in which they take such temporal and carnal delight. And at an hour of which they are unaware, and are living in great sin, I shall then snatch them away from earthly life and put them to eternal death in a place where they will nevermore see my face, because they loved to do and accomplish their corrupted will rather than perform my will and my commandments."

After these things had thus been seen and heard, this vision disappeared.

Book 7:28   The Virgin Mary complains of Neapolitans who own slaves and rely on fortune-tellers
Naples, February 1373

A revelation of the Virgin Mary to Lady Bridget in the city of Naples, directed to Lord Bernard, the Neapolitan archbishop. The revelation reproaches those who do not instruct their servants or slaves, newly converted to the faith, in the Catholic faith and Christian law. The Virgin Mary also reproves those masters who maltreat their servants and tries their patience beyond measure. She also threatens with great punishment fortune-tellers, enchanters and diviners and also those who support them and put faith in them.

Bridget writes to Lord Bernard, archbishop of Naples, saying: "Reverend Father and Lord! When that person, whom you know well, was praying in a rapture of contemplation, the Virgin Mary appeared to her and said to her this: 'I, who speak to you, am the Queen of heaven. I am, as it were, a gardener of this world. For when a gardener sees the rise of a strong wind harmful to the little plants and the trees of his garden, at once he runs to them quickly and binds them fast with sturdy stakes as well as he can. And thus he comes to their aid, in various ways according to his ability, lest they be broken or uprooted by the rushing wind.

'I, the Mother of mercy, do the same in the garden of this world. For when I see blowing on the hearts of human beings the dangerous winds of the devil's temptations and wicked suggestions, at once I have recourse to my Lord and my God, my Son Jesus Christ, helping them with my prayers and obtaining from him his outpouring of the Holy

Spirit into their hearts to support and strengthen them, that they may be kept spiritually uninjured by the diabolic wind of temptations, lest the devil prevail against human beings, breaking their souls and plucking them up by the stem in accordance with his wicked desire.

'And thus when, with humility of heart human beings receive these supports of mine and my assistance, at once they are defended against the diabolic onslaught of temptation and, remaining firm in the state of grace, they bear for God and for me the fruit of sweetness in due season. But as for those who scorn the aforesaid spiritual support of my Son and me and are swayed by the wind of temptations through consent to the devil and through their wrong actions, they are uprooted from the state of grace and, through sinful desires and deeds, are led by the devil to the profound and eternal pain and darkness of hell. Now, however, know that in the Neapolitan citizenry many different horrible and secret sins are being committed which I will not relate to you. But instead I am speaking to you now about two kinds of open sins that greatly displease my Son and me, and all the heavenly court.

'The first sin is the fact that in this said city many citizens buy pagans and infidels to be their slaves, and that some masters of these slaves do not bother to baptize them and do not want to convert them to the Christian faith. And even if some of them are baptized, their masters do not have them instructed and trained in the Christian faith or train them in the reception of the Church's sacraments, any more than they did before the slaves' baptism and conversion. And so the converted slaves, after accepting the faith, commit many sins and do not know how to return to the sacraments of penance and Communion or how to be restored to a state of salvation and of reconciliation with God.

'Moreover, some keep their female servants and slaves in extreme abjection and degradation, as if they were dogs—selling them and, what is worse, frequently sending them to a brothel to earn money, which is a disgrace and an abomination. Others, in fact, keep them in their own houses as prostitutes both for themselves and for others; and this is hateful to God and to me, and also to the whole heavenly court.

'Some other masters grieve and abuse their servants with cruel words and blows, so that some of them come close to a state of despair and want to kill themselves. These sins and acts of negligence much displease God and all the heavenly court.

'For God himself loves them because he created them; and to save all, he came into the world, taking flesh from me, and endured suffering and death on the cross. Know too that if anyone buys such pagans with the intention of making them Christians and wants to instruct and train them in Christian faith and virtue and intends, during his life or at his death, to set these slaves at liberty so that the slaves may not pass to his heirs, such a master of slaves merits much by this and is acceptable in the sight of God. But know for certain that those who do the contrary will be heavily punished by God.

'The second kind of sin is that many men and women, of various standings in the community, keep about them and consult wicked fortune-tellers and diviners and the most evil of enchantresses. For sometimes they ask them to perform witchcraft and incantations in order that they may be able to conceive and beget children. Others require them to perform incantations and to make fetishes that will cause certain men and women, or even their temporal lords, to be enamoured of them to the point of distraction and to love them with all their heart. Others, in fact, beg foreknowledge of the future from these same accursed witches.

'Many others ask them to give them healing of their infirmities through their arts of enchantment and witchcraft. All indeed who keep and consult such people and follow their wicked advice and diabolic remedies, and, indeed, all the diviners and enchantresses who promise the things mentioned above—all are cursed and hateful in the sight of God.

'As long as they continue in such a state, no infusion of the Holy Spirit will ever enter their hearts. Nevertheless, if they repent and humbly amend their lives with the true intent of not falling back into the same sin again, they will obtain grace and mercy from my Son.'"

When these things had been heard, this vision disappeared.

Book 7:30   Bridget conveys Jesus' judgement over Naples
Naples, March 1373

I saw a grand palace set, as it were, in the serene sky. In it was the host of the heavenly army, innumerable as the atoms of the sun, gleaming as of the sun's rays. But in the palace, on a wonderful throne there sat the figure of a human being, a Lord of incomprehensible beauty and immense power; his clothes were of inexpressible brightness. And before him who sat on the throne there stood a Virgin who was more radiant than the sun.

All the heavenly host, who stood nearby, reverently honoured her as the queen of heaven. But then he who sat on the throne opened his mouth and said: "Hearken, all you my enemies who live in the world; for to my friends who follow my will, I am not speaking. Hearken, all you clerics: archbishops and bishops and all of lower rank in the Church! Hearken, all you religious, of whatever order you are! Hearken, you kings and princes and judges of the earth and all you who serve!

"Hearken, you women: princesses and all ladies and maidservants! All you inhabitants of the world, of whatever condition or rank you are, whether great or small, hearken to these words that I myself, who created you, now speak to you! I complain because you have withdrawn from me and have put faith in the devil, my enemy. You have abandoned my commandments; you follow the will of the devil and you obey his suggestions.

"You do not attend to the fact that I, the unchanging and eternal God, your Creator, came down from heaven, was born of a Virgin and lived with you. Through my own self, I opened the way for you by which you might go to heaven. I was stripped and scourged and crowned with thorns and so forcefully crucified on the cross that all the sinews and joints of my body were torn apart. I heard all insults and endured a contemptible death and the most bitter heartache for the sake of your salvation.

"To all these things, O my enemies, you are not attentive because you have been deceived. Therefore you bear the yoke and burden of the devil with false ease, and neither know nor feel the approach of sorrow caused by the interminable burden that you carry. Nor is this enough for you; for your pride is so great that if you could ascend above me, you would gladly do it. And the pleasure of the flesh is so important to you that you would more gladly forfeit me than give up your carnal delight.

"Moreover, your greed is as insatiable as a sack with a hole in it; for there is nothing that can satisfy your greed. Therefore, I swear by my Godhead that if you die in the state in which you now are, you shall never see my face; but for your pride you shall sink so deeply into hell that all the devils will be above you, afflicting you beyond all consolation. Indeed, for your lust you shall be filled with horrible diabolic venom; and for your greed you shall be filled with sorrow and anguish; and you shall be partakers of all the evil that there is in hell.

"O my enemies—abominable and ungrateful and degenerate—I seem to you, as it were, a worm dead in winter. Therefore, you do whatever things you will, and you prosper. But I will arise, as it were, in summer and then you shall be silent, and you shall not escape my hand. But nevertheless, O my enemies, because I have redeemed you with my blood and because I am in quest of naught but your souls, return to me even now with humility and I will gladly receive you as my children. Shake from you the devil's heavy yoke and recall my charity and you shall see in your conscience that I am sweet and meek."

Book 4:141   Christ urges Pope Gregory XI to return to Rome
Naples, 26 January 1373, St Polycarp's Day

Christ appeared to Lady Bridget while she was praying for Pope Gregory XI. He said to her: "Listen carefully, my daughter, to what I tell you. Understand that this Pope Gregory is like a paralytic who cannot use his hands to work or his feet to walk. The disease of paralysis is produced by corrupt blood and humour, and by cold. In the same way, an immoderate love of himself and the coldness of his tepid mind toward me keep this pope encumbered, as it were. Understand, however, that, by the help of the Virgin Mary, my Mother, he is already beginning to move his hands and feet, that is, to act after my will and for my honour by coming to Rome. Be thus assured that he will come to Rome and initiate the way to future good there, though he will not finish it."

Lady Bridget then answered: "The Lord, my God, the queen of Naples and many others tell me that it is impossible for Pope Gregory to come to Rome, because the king of France and the cardinals and others are putting as many obstacles as they can in his way. I have heard that many people have arisen there saying that they have God's Spirit and receive divine revelations and visions that they use as a pretext to dissuade him from coming. Therefore I am very much afraid that his coming will be prevented."

God answered: "You have heard it read how Jeremiah lived in Israel in those days and had God's Spirit for prophecy, and how there were many at the time who had the spirit of dreams and lies. The wicked king put his trust in them, which is why both the king himself and his people fell into captivity. If the king had put his trust in Jeremiah alone, my anger would have been withdrawn from him. So it is now. Sages arise or dreamers or friends, not of the spirit but of the flesh, and they use their persuasion on Pope Gregory and dissuade him from the opposite course of action. Nevertheless, I, the Lord, shall still prevail over them and bring the pope to Rome against their encouragement. However, whether you will see him come or not, is not permitted for you to know."

Book 4:142   Christ urges Pope Gregory XI to return to Rome
Naples, February 1373, handed to the pope in July 1373

Holy Father, that person whom Your Holiness knows well was praying in vigil when she fell into a spiritual rapture of contemplation. She saw in spirit the likeness of a throne on which was seated the likeness of a man of inestimable beauty, a lord of unfathomable might. A great multitude of saints and a countless host of angels stood around the throne. A bishop dressed in pontifical regalia stood at some distance before the throne.

The lord who was seated on the throne spoke to me and said: "All power in heaven and on earth has been given to me by my Father. Although I seem to be speaking to you with one mouth, I do not speak alone, for the Father and the Holy Spirit speak with me. We three persons are one in the substance of the divinity."

Then he addressed the bishop and said: "Listen, Pope Gregory, to the eleven points I say to you, and attend carefully to what I tell you! Why do you hate me so? For what reason is your audacity and presumption so great against me? Your worldly court is plundering my heavenly court. In your pride you are robbing me of my sheep. You unjustly extort and steal the ecclesiastical property that belongs to me as well as the possessions of the subjects of my church, and you give them to your temporal friends. You take and unjustly receive goods from my poor and distribute them dishonourably to your rich. Accordingly, your audacity and presumption are exceedingly great, for you enter into my court so rashly and show no consideration for what is mine.

"What have I done to you, Gregory? I patiently allowed you to rise to the pontificate. I explained my will to you beforehand by means of letters transmitted to you by divine revelation from Rome. I admonished you through them for the sake of your soul's salvation, and I warned you in them about your great losses. How have you repaid me for all these benefits? What are you doing about the fact that great pride rules in your court, and insatiable greed and detestable luxury and even the evil ruin of horrible simony?

"Furthermore, you are stealing and plundering countless souls away from me. You cast into the fire of Gehenna nearly all those who come to your court, simply because you do not take diligent care of the things pertaining to my court, though you are the prelate and shepherd of my sheep. It is therefore your fault, because you do not prudently consider what must be done or corrected for their spiritual salvation.

"Though I could justly condemn you for all the aforesaid, yet I am again admonishing you out of mercy for the salvation of your soul to come to your see in Rome as soon as you can. I leave the time up to you. Know, though, that the more you delay, the greater will be the decrease in your spiritual and moral development. The sooner you come to Rome, the sooner you will experience an increase of virtue and of the gifts of the Holy Spirit, and the more you will be inflamed with the divine fire of my love. Come, then, and do not delay! Come not with your customary pride and worldly pomp, but with all humility and ardent love!

"As soon as you have thus come, uproot, pluck out and destroy all the vices of your court! Separate yourself from the counsel of carnal-minded and worldly friends and follow humbly the spiritual counsel of my friends. Approach, then, and be not afraid. Get up like a man and clothe yourself confidently in strength!

"Start to reform the Church that I purchased with my own blood, in order that it may be reformed and led back spiritually to its pristine state of holiness, for nowadays more veneration is shown to a brothel than to my Holy Church.

"If you do not obey this my will, then you can be quite sure that you will be condemned by me before all my heavenly court with the same kind of sentence and spiritual justice with which one condemns and punishes a worldly prelate that is to be stripped of his rank. He is publicly divested of his sacred pontifical garb, defeated and accursed. He is filled with ignominy and shame. This is what I will do to you. I shall send you away from the glory of heaven. Everything that now gives you peace and honour will then be turned into a curse and your eternal shame. Every demon in hell will snatch a piece of your soul, immortal and indestructible as it is, and you will be filled with an everlasting curse instead of a blessing.

"For as long as I still tolerate your disobedience, you will still prosper. However, Gregory, my son, I admonish you again to convert to me with humility. Heed my counsel. I am your Father and Creator. If you obey me in what I have told you, I will welcome you mercifully like a loving father. Bravely approach the way of justice and you shall prosper. Do not despise the one who loves you. If you obey, I will show you mercy and bless and adorn you with the precious pontifical regalia of a true pope. I shall clothe you with myself in such a way that you will be in me and I in you, and you shall be glorified in eternity."

After this had been seen and heard, the vision faded.

Book 4:143   Christ urges Pope Gregory XI to return to Rome
Fourth revelation in the same subject filed in Naples in February 1373 and handed over to the pope in July 1373

Our Lord Jesus Christ told me, Reverend Bishop, to write you the following words for you to show to the pope. "The Pope seeks a sign. Tell him that the pharisees sought a sign and that I answered them that, just as Jonah was in the belly of the whale for three days and nights, so I, the Virgin's Son, was dead in the earth for three days and nights. After the promised sign, I, God's Son, suffered, died and was buried, and rose again and ascended into my glory. Thus, Pope Gregory has received the sign of my exhortation to save souls. Let him do with deeds what belongs to my honour. Let him struggle to save souls and return my Church to its pristine state. Then he will experience the sign and reward of eternal consolation. He will also have a second sign. If he does not obey my words and come to Italy, he will lose not only temporal goods but also spiritual ones, and he will feel troubled at heart so long as he lives. Though his heart may sometimes seem to have some relief, the remorse of his conscience and his inner troubles will stay with him. The third sign is that I, God, speak miraculously to a woman. What is the purpose of this? What is the benefit of it, if not the salvation and good of souls and the reformation of the wicked and the improvement of the good?

"Concerning the dispute between the pope and Barnabò, I answer that it is loathsome to me beyond measure, for numberless souls are in peril because of it. It is therefore my will that they should reach an agreement. Even if the pope were to be expelled from his papacy, it would be better for him to humble himself and come to an agreement, should the occasion present itself, than to allow so many souls to perish in eternal damnation. Concerning the betterment of the kingdom of France, it will not be made known until the pope himself arrives in Italy.

"It is as though there were a gibbet from which hung a rope that a numberless crowd was pulling to one side while only one man was pulling it to the other. So it is with the damnation of souls. A great many are working on it. This pope should gaze on me alone, though everyone else is dissuading him from coming to Rome and resisting it as much as they can. He should trust in me alone, and I will help him, and none of them will prevail over him. As chicks in a nest raise themselves up and clamour and rejoice when their mother comes, so I shall joyfully run out to meet him and raise him up and honour him in both soul and body."

The Lord spoke again: "Because the pope is in doubt as to whether he should come to Rome for sake of the re-establishment of the peace and of my Church, I will that he should come next autumn. Let him know that he can do nothing more pleasing to me than to come to Italy."

Extravagantes 110 Bridget considers the appropriateness of receiving a monetary gift from the queen

Naples, March 1373

When St Bridget was on her way back to Rome from the holy city of Jerusalem, a queen, moved by compassion, handed her a certain amount of money in the city of Naples, for help and maintenance. As she wondered if she should receive such a gift, Christ revealed himself to her and said, "Is it not good to pay friendship with enmity and good with evil? And don't you put snow in a cold container, so that it gets even colder? Admittedly, although the queen gave you what she offered with a cold heart, receive it with love and reverence and pray for her to reach the divine heart, for it is written that the abundance of others should replace the poor of the poor, and that no one's good deeds shall be forgotten before God."

Book 7:31 Christ predicts Bridget's death

Bridget's final revelation, Rome, 18 July 1373

It happened five days before Lady Bridget died that our Lord Jesus Christ appeared to her in front of the altar that stood in her chamber. He showed himself with a joyful face and said to her: "I have done to you what a bridegroom usually does, concealing himself from his bride so that he may be more ardently desired by her. Thus I have not visited you with consolations during this time; for it was the time of your testing.

"Therefore, now that you have already been tested, go forward and prepare yourself; for now is the time for the fulfilment of that which I promised you: namely, that before my altar you shall be clothed and consecrated as a nun. And henceforth you shall be counted, not only as my bride, but also as a nun and a mother in Vadstena. Nevertheless, know that you will lay down your body here in Rome until it comes to the place prepared for it. For it pleases me to spare you from your labours and to accept your will in place of the completed action."

And having turned toward Rome, he said as if making a complaint: "O my Rome, O my Rome, the pope scorns you and does not attend to my words but accepts the doubtful in place of the certain. Therefore he shall hear my voice no more; for he makes the time of my mercy dependent on his own choice."

Then he said to the bride: "As for you, however: tell the prior to hand over all these words of mine, in all the revelations, to the brothers and to my bishop, to whom I shall give the fervour of my Spirit and whom I shall fill with my grace. And know that when it so pleases me, those human beings will come who will receive those words of the heavenly revelations with sweetness and joy that up until now have been made only to you; and all the things that have been said to you will be accomplished.

"And although my grace has been withdrawn from many because of their ingratitude, nevertheless others will come in their place who will obtain my grace. But among the very last words of the revelations made to you, include the common and universal revelation that I gave to you in Naples. For my judgement shall be carried out on all the nations who do not humbly return to me, as it has been shown to you."

However, after these and many other things not written here had been said, Bridget made mention of and arrangements for some persons living with her who, before death, she said she had seen in God's presence.

After those things had been heard, the Lord added these words: "On the morning of the fifth day, after you have received the sacraments, call together one by one the persons who are present and living with you and who I have just named to you, and tell them the things that they must do. And thus, amidst these words and their hands, you will come to your monastery, into my joy; and your body will be placed in Vadstena."

Then, as the fifth day approached, at the moment of dawn, Christ appeared to her again and consoled her. But when Mass had been said and after she had received the sacraments with very great devotion and reverence, in the hands of the aforesaid persons she sent forth her spirit.

Chronological overview over Bridget's life

1303 Bridget is born in Finsta, Uppland.

1314 Her mother, Ingeborg Bengtsdotter, dies. Bridget moves to the home of her Aunt Katarina Bengtsdotter on the farm Aspanäs in Malexander.

1316 Bridget marries 18-year-old Ulf Gudsmarsson, later the governor of Närke. The couple move to Ulvåsa, at the Lake Boren.

1319–37 The children Märta, Gudmar, Karl, Ingeborg, Catherine, Birger, Bengt and Cecilia are born.

1327 Bridget's father, Birger Persson, the governor in Uppland, dies.

1335 Bridget becomes court lady of Queen Blanka.

1337 The Hundred Years' War breaks out between England and France and continues until 1453.

1339 Bridget and Ulf go on a pilgrimage to the tomb of St Olof in Nidaros, Norway.

1341–42 Bridget and Ulf go on a pilgrimage to the tomb of St James in Santiago de Compostela in Galicia.

1342 Bridget and Ulf return from the pilgrimage and settle in the Alvastra monastery.

1344 Ulf dies and Bridget stays in the Alvastra monastery's annex.

1348 Bridget, through the bishop of Turku, submits a revelation to the pope in Avignon as well as to the kings of England and France in order to bring peace between the two countries.

1349 Bridget travels to Rome.

1350s and 1360s Bridget visits Naples, Bari, Assisi and other places in Italy.

1367–70 Pope Urban V moves to Rome and then returns to Avignon.

1370 Urban V approves Bridget's monastic rule by taking over the Augustinian rule on 3 August.

1371–73 Pilgrimage to the Holy Land.

1373 Bridget dies in her residence in Rome on 23 July.

1373 On 8 December, the funeral procession to Vadstena bearing Bridget's remains starts.

1374 Bridget's remains are deposited in Vadstena on 4 July.

1377 Pope Gregory XI returns to Rome and thus ends the papal "Babylonian captivity".

1378 Bridget's monastic rule is confirmed.

1391 Bridget is proclaimed a saint on 7 October by Pope Boniface IX.

1420 Pope Martin V confirms Bridget's sanctification.

1999 Bridget is proclaimed the patron saint of Europe on 1 October, with Catherine of Siena and Edith Stein.

Bridgettine guesthouses mentioned in the book

Details are correct at the time of going to print.

Rome

Casa di Santa Brigida,
Piazza Farnese 96, 00186 Roma (Italy)
Telephone: +390668892596
Email: casabrigidaroma@brigidine.org
Website: www.casabrigidaroma.it

Naples

Eremo SS. Salvatore
Via dell'Eremo 87, 80131 Camaldoli Napoli (Italy)
Telephone: +390815872519
e-mail: eremo.camaldoli@libero.it
Website: www.casabrigidacamaldoli.it

Jerusalem

John Paul II Center for Interreligious Dialogue
Mount of Olives, Al Sowaneh, 91191 Jerusalem (Israel)
Telephone: +97226281801
e-mail: birgitjerusalem@014.net.il
Website: www.bridgettinesistersjerusalem.wordpress.com

Bethlehem

Mary's House The Bridgettine Sisters
Salesian Street, Bethlehem (Palestinian territory)
Telephone: +97022750360
Email: bridgetabet@gmail.com
Website: www.brigidine.org/case/betlemme.php

Vadstena

S:ta Birgittas kloster Pax Marie
Myntbacken 2, 592 30 Vadstena (Sweden)
Telephone: +4614310943
Email: guesthouse@birgittakloster.se
Website: www.birgittaskloster.se